Amazin' Mets

The Miracle of '69

DAILY  NEWS

Sports Publishing Inc.
www.SportsPublishingInc.com

Other Daily News Books

Jets: Broadway's 30-Year Guarantee
Big Town/Big Time: A New York Epic 1898-1998
Joe DiMaggio: An American Icon
Yogi Berra: An American Original
Yankees '98: Best Ever

DAILY ⊚ NEWS

Coordinating editor: Vincent Panzarino
Developmental editor: Terrence C. Miltner
Editor: Susan M. McKinney
Production coordinator: Erin J. Sands
Book layout: Erin J. Sands
Interior design: Jennifer L. Polson
Cover design: Terry N. Hayden
Photo editor: Vincent Panzarino
Proofreader: David Hamburg

Front cover photos: Paul DeMaria & Ed Clarity/*The New York Daily News*
Back cover photo: Courtesy of the New York Mets

Front row (l. to r.): Trainer Gus Mauch, coaches Joe Pignatano, Rube Walker, Yogi Berra and Eddie Yost, assistant trainer Joe Deer.

Second row: Tug McGraw, Gary Gentry, Al Weis, Cleon Jones, manager Gil Hodges, Jerry Grote, Bud Harrelson, Ed Charles, Rod Gaspar and Duffy Dyer.

Third row : Jim McAndrew, Tommie Agee, Cal Koonce, Ken Boswell, Tom Seaver, Jerry Koosman, Ron Swoboda, Wayne Garrett, Bobby Pfeil and traveling secretary Lou Niss.

Fourth row: Equipment manager Nick Torman, J.C. Martin, Ron Taylor, Ed Kranepool, Don Cardwell, Donn Clendenon, Nolan Ryan, Art Shamsky, Jack DiLauro and clubhouse attendant Roy Neuer.

ISBN: 1-58261-297-8
Library of Congress Catalog Number: 00-101219

Printed in the United States.

SPORTS PUBLISHING INC.
www.SportsPublishingInc.com

Table of Contents

Acknowledgments

It was a routine fly ball to left field, routinely fielded by Cleon Jones. A routine finish to a season that was anything but routine.

The New York Mets had been "Amazin'" for seven years after they brought National League baseball back to New York City in 1962, amazingly bad, that is. They lost 120 games the first year and were last in the National League for six years straight.

In 1968 they were ninth and in 1969 they were guaranteed to be no worse than sixth. That was because both the National and American Leagues were expanded to 12 teams and two divisions.

In 1969 there was a different kind of amazing to document. The Mets opened their season with a loss, but there were real differences between this Mets team and the teams that had come before. This team had the strongest pitching staff in the National League, led by young superstars Tom Seaver and Jerry Koosman. The Mets also had the hitting to back up their ace pitching staff. As the Mets set milestone after milestone on their way to the World Series, the *Daily News* was there to document every pitch, every hit, and every run.

This book would not have happened if not for the overwhelming support of Ed Fay (VP/Director of Editorial Administration) and Les Goodstein (Executive Vice President/Associate Publisher) of the *Daily News*.

The book would not have been as thorough if not for the devotion of Vincent Panzarino. His extensive search through the *Daily News* archives and his perspective as a devoted fan of the 1969 Mets gave the book a feel that only a true fan could convey. Others who were instrumental in making this project such a success include Lenore Schlossberg, John Polizano, Eric Meskauskas, Mike Lipack, Bill Martin, Angela Troisi, Faigi Rosenthal, Dawn Jackson and Scott Browne. From the *Daily News* sports department, I specifically want to acknowledge the support of editors Barry Werner and Leon Carter.

Space limitations preclude us from thanking each and every writer and photographer whose work appears in this book. However, wherever available, we have preserved the writers' bylines and the photographers' credits to ensure proper attribution for their work.

And finally, I am grateful for the support and hard work of those at Sports Publishing Inc. My gratitude goes to Susan McKinney, Jennifer Polson, Erin Prescher, and Terry Hayden for all of their hard work on the production of the book, and to Joseph Bannon Jr., Tom Bast, Jeff Ellish and Joanna Wright for their guidance and feedback on this project.

Terrence C. Miltner
Developmental Editor

Foreword

by Ed Kranepool

The Amazin' Mets, the winningest losers in the history of baseball, started their first home series in 1962 on Friday the 13th. A little over 13,000 people — including myself, who was a guest of the Mets—watched the return of the senior circuit to New York City. The Mets lost their home opener, 4-3, in what was to become typically poor Met play over the next 7 1/2 years.

On June 27, 1962, I signed a contract with the Mets to fulfill a lifelong dream to be a major leaguer. A week after signing the contract, I joined the Mets on a West Coast trip. On my first night as a Met, Sandy Koufax pitched a no hitter against us and struck out 18 men (nine in a row to start the game). What a welcome to the major leagues.

The Lovable Mets went on to set records for losses in 1962 and the following season. Only Casey Stengel's "Stengelese" and the continuous player changes kept the interest of the fans through the long summer days. Casey was the only bright spot. His wit and wisdom kept us going.

Shea Stadium was completed in 1964 and marked the beginning of a new era. Young players like Bud Harrelson, Ron Swoboda and Dick Selma brought the average age of our roster down, but nothing changed. Nine days into the season we grabbed last place and held firmly onto it for the rest of the way. By July 31, 1964, the Mets were 30 games behind and the team's revolving-door policy continued. Players would take all of their clothes with them on road trips because they knew they might not be coming back to New York. The highlight of the '65 season was Tug McGraw's victory over Sandy Koufax.

In 1966, the roster underwent continuous change, with half the players on the opening-day roster never wearing a Mets uniform. From the players' viewpoint, this was getting old. We never knew the players without a scorecard. Wes Westrum took over in 1966, and his positive approach set a tone that would be built upon by Gil Hodges, who took over the Mets for the 1968 season. Gil was just what the doctor ordered.

A born leader, Gil changed the direction of the ballclub and installed a positive attitude from the first day of spring training. Gil was a stickler for details and the proper way of playing the game. You either played his way or you hit the highway. He wanted his hitters to be more aggressive and worked hard in spring training on fundamentals and tight defense. The '68 season ended with the Mets winning 73 games and the hope of good things to come.

In 1969, with the Las Vegas odds at 100-1 for the Mets to win the pennant, few were expecting a miracle by the Mets. However, we knew we had first-rate coaches, good young players with potential and a core of experienced veterans. With baseball's realignment to divisional play, we knew we could finish no lower than sixth, and probably fifth, as the Expos joined the National League that season.

With strong pitching, solid defense and a firm belief in Gil's approach to the game, we knew we could be competitive. But a World Series? The front office thought we were a player short, and so we traded for Donn Clendenon. Donn was good for the club both on the field and in the clubhouse. Before Donn joined the team, we set out for a road trip to California.

Having only won the occasional game in California in years past, our sweep of all three teams on that trip instilled a new confidence in the clubhouse. As our confidence grew, our play improved. From there, down the stretch, we felt there was no one who could beat us. From there, the sky was the limit.

What a wonderful change from my rookie year, when there was a feeling that there wasn't anyone who couldn't beat us. At the end of the season—having beaten everyone—we stood forever as baseball's most amazing World Series champions.

This book celebrates the life long dream of every player who ever played the game of baseball.

The World Champion New York Mets make their way through a blizzard of ticker tape on lower Broadway on their way up the Canyon of Heroes to City Hall.

Mets manager Gil Hodges gets a catcher's-eye view of batting practice during a workout at the St. Petersburg training camp.

Preseason

'69

Before the New York Mets could begin their Miracle Season, there would have to be a Major League Baseball Season. The season was placed in jeopardy when the owners and players tried to re-negotiate contributions to the players' pension from television revenues. The previous agreement had expired, and both sides were looking to improve their positions.

As the opening of spring training neared, some players crossed the picket line, signed their contracts, and began preparing for the season. The owners and players finally reached a compromise, and spring training got started with a minimal delay.

The Mets made sure they had a pair of aces up manager Gil Hodges' sleeve; both Tom Seaver and Jerry Koosman were given raises. But the rest of the deck was full of wild cards as Hodges began his second season at the Mets' helm—and his first season after a heart attack in September of '68.

Even without the labor dispute, this was going to be like no season that had ever been played before. With the addition of two teams to the American League, and the addition of the Montreal Expos and San Diego Padres to the National League, both leagues split into two divisions for the first time. The winners of each division would meet in a best-of-five playoff to decide who carried the NL and the AL pennants to the World Series.

Vegas bookmakers didn't think much of the Mets' chances and made them 100-to-1 odds to win the National League pennant.

1962:
A Year to Remember

The baseball world had never seen anything like it. At least Casey Stengel hadn't, and he'd been around the baseball world for a couple of lifetimes.

"Can't anybody here play this game?" the Ol' Perfessor asked when he got a good look at his 1962 Mets. The answer to his question was, without exaggeration, no.

The newborn Mets of '62 were losers, all right, but not ordinary losers—they were hopeless with a flair that went straight to the schmaltzy spot in New York's heart. Baseball-undernourished National League fans traveled to see the team in huge numbers that bitter-sweet year. The Mets fed them gruel and the fans loved it.

To the Polo Grounds they came, carrying banners shrieking everything from encouragement to vilification and quite a lot of very funny things in between. It soon became clear that whatever humiliations the ballclub might be suffering, the fans were having a helluva good time.

Maybe it was the year the anit-hero was born; certainly the Mets had plenty of them. Most famous of all, of course, was the king of the clumsies, known as Marvelous Marv Throneberry. The quintessential Met, heavy-footed Marv was probably good for more

> It soon became clear that what-ever humiliations the ballclub might be suffering, the fans were having a helluva good time.

laughs that year than Nichols and May. Even the team's owner, Mrs. Joan Payson, had to chuckle.

The antiheroes were legion as well as legend. There was Hot Rod Kanehl, who played every position, or was it that every position played him? There was Don Zimmer, who established a solid basis for anonymity by going 0-for-34 at the plate during one stretch before being traded off to the Reds for Cliff Cook.

There were Roger Craig, the Mets' first 24-game loser, and Charley Neal, who suddenly forgot how to field grounders when he became a Met.

And there were Elio Chacon, the no-field, no-hit, no-talk Latin, and the two Bob Millers that no one could keep straight, probably because they didn't have any particular reason to. And there were Craig Anderson and Al Jackson and the one Met pitcher with a winning record, Ken MacKenzie (5-4). And don't forget Felix Mantilla, Frank Thomas and Chris Cannizzaro.

The fans came to see them all, for better or for worse—and it was worse than anyone could have

Four newly minted New York Mets, (l to r) Frank Thomas, Gil Hodges, Don Zimmer and Roger Craig, celebrate the opening of the season. Beyond Opening Day, there was little to celebrate.

imagined. The final statistics were brutal—120 team losses, with losing streaks of nine, 11, 13 and 17 games in a row that year, and their slap-hapless pitching staff threw 192 home run balls and allowed an average of 5.04 earned runs.

Still, it's doubtful that 922,530 people ever had more fun at a ballpark than the Met customers of '62.

Those were the days. ■

1962 National League Standings

	Wins	Losses	Pct.	G.B.
1. San Francisco	103	62	.624	—
2. Los Angeles	102	63	.618	1
3. Cincinnati	98	64	.605	3 1/2
4. Pittsburgh	93	68	.578	8
5. Milwaukee	86	76	.531	15 1/2
6. St. Louis	84	78	.519	17 1/2
7. Philadelphia	81	80	.503	20
8. Houston	64	96	.400	36 1/2
9. Chicago	59	103	.634	42 1/2
10. New York	40	120	.250	60 1/2

preseason '69

NL OKs 2 Divisions for '69 as Mets Capitulate

by Dick Young

A *long-distance phone call to Mrs. Payson broke the stalemate at the tedious NL meeting here today and led to the acceptance of divisional play for 1969. Mets owner Joan Payson, contacted in Maine by Don Grant, agreed to give in, and thus the Nationals aligned their clubs into six-team divisions as the AL has done.*

When the AL split into sixes in May, the NL announced it would stick with one 12-team setup. However, under prodding by Commissioner Eckert and the executive committee, the Nationals agreed to a compromise formula: They would split if the AL would abandon its proposed 156-game schedule and return to 162. In the interest of uniformity, the Americans today agreed.

Thus, a tentative 1969 calendar has been set up as follows: Regular schedule to commence Monday, April 7, and end Thursday, October 2. Playoffs to start Saturday, October 4, and run concurrently. World Series to start Saturday, October 11, and how about that, Mr. Rozelle?

Both leagues adopted the same formula for divisional play. It is called the 9-6 plan. Each club plays others in its division 9 games at home and 9 away, for a total of 90; 6 at home, 6 away against the teams in the other division, for a total of 72. Grand total: 162. The playoffs between top-finishing teams will be best 3-of-5 in both leagues.

So, the Giants and Dodgers will come to Shea for only 6 games each instead of 9 as presently. That was the bone of Don Grant's resistance. The Mets' board chairman claims he previously had been promised a compromise whereby the Dodgers would remain in the Mets' division and only the Giants would be lost for the three extra games.

"I came to Houston with that understanding." said Grant. "But when I got here, I found out otherwise."

Grant resisted the switch. Through long, sometimes harsh debate; through "six or seven votes" by his own count, Grant rejected the groupings. In as much as unanimity is required in the NL, the meeting went on.

Finally, Grant asked to be permitted to make a phone call. He left the room and placed the call to Mrs. Payson. "I'm sorry you have to go through it," he later quoted her as telling him, "but I'll go along with whatever you do."

Given that release by his boss, Grant returned to the room and voted yes.

"I'm stubborn, but not bullheaded," he said. ■

preseason '69

Baseball's Great Divide

National League

East

New York
Montreal
Philadelphia
Pittsburgh
Chicago
St. Louis

West

San Francisco
Los Angeles
San Diego
Houston
Cincinnati
Atlanta

American League

East

New York
Washington
Boston
Cleveland
Detroit
Baltimore

West

Minnesota
Chicago
Oakland
Kansas City
Seattle
California

Mets owner Joan Payson appears apprehensive while watching her team play.

preseason '69

It's 3-and-2 on the Baseball Season

Time runs short as players threaten to strike out 1969

by Jerry Lisker

Imagine baseball without Pete Rose, Carl Yastrzemski, Juan Marichal, Bob Gibson or Willie Mays? Imagine no baseball at all?

Sounds crazy, eh? Don't laugh, it could happen, and it is coming precariously close to becoming a fact. Unless there's some legitimate head-to-head bargaining between the baseball owners and the Players Association real soon, there might not be a baseball season. The players will be on strike. Yes, strike. A naughty word in sports.

What's the problem? The answer is money, pension money. On January 17, Marvin Miller, the attorney for the Players Association, revealed a poll showing the players overwhelmingly rejected an offer by the owners to increase the players' pension fund by a million dollars a year.

Everyone who is anyone in baseball signed his name: Hank Aaron, Lou Brock, Orlando Cepeda, Frank Howard, Brooks and Frank Robinson, Mickey Mantle, Al Kaline and Harmon Killebrew. They all affixed their John Hancocks.

No contract means no reporting to spring training. No spring training may very well mean no baseball, or a screwed up season at best.

Here's the big problem between the Players Association and the owners:

The owners want to change the pension money they contribute from a percentage basis to a cash basis. The original pension contracts—two five-year pacts '57-'62 and '62-'67—specified that 60% of the World Series TV revenue and 95% of the All-Star TV loot and all the net gate receipts go into the pension fund. Last year the contract was carried over by mutual agreement.

Now, the owners have decided they would rather pay the lump sum of one

Marvin Miller

million into the pension fund and forget about the TV dough. A fixed sum of a million, payable every year regardless of what the TV percentage comes to, is what the owners feel is a fair contribution.

Understandably, the players stand to gain more money on a percentage basis than they would on a flat contribution from the owners. The current TV-radio World Series and All-Star game package is with NBC. The three-year contract, beginning this year, carries a price tag of $45.3 million. That's a lot of commercials. ■

preseason '69

Mets to Play 'Em Anyway

by Dick Young

Johnny Murphy today stated that the Mets will go ahead with their exhibition schedule, employing whatever players are on hand.

Commissioner Bowie Kuhn, who dropped into camp here before flying back to New York for consultation with the warring principals, said he expected the exhibition schedule to be played, but added: "Of course, we must be careful to see that the public is not deceived or misled about what they are paying for in such games. I'm sure they will realize what the situation is."

Murphy expressed the viewpoint that exhibition games are played to get in shape and to try out rookies for positions on the club. "Maybe we'll find we have some kids here who are better than the ones we've been playing," he said.

Tom Seaver showed up for a chat with Murphy but did not work out. "I just wanted Mr. Murphy to know how I thought about this thing," said Seaver.

He grinned and said, "I have to be off now to run my camp."

Seaver is conducting conditioning sessions for boycotting ballplayers. He, Jerry Koosman, Al Jackson and Bud Harrelson work out daily in a playground near Seaver's apartment. "We're running, playing catch and doing some situps," said Seaver. "We'll be ready when the time comes." ∎

Bulletin:

February 25, 1969
by Joe Trimble

An agreement to settle the players' boycott against major league baseball was reached shortly before midnight, it was learned tonight.

Day-long meetings between the Major League Players Assn. and representatives of the owners produced the agreement, details of which will be made in joint announcement tomorrow afternoon.

As part of the agreement, all players will be asked to negotiate contracts at once and, if satisfied, proceed to training camps immediately.

The settlement needs only approval of both sides and such approval had already been assured.

The driving force behind the settlement was Commissioner Bowie Kuhn, who had flown to New York Sunday from St. Petersburg, Florida. Kuhn instructed the warring factions to remain in session until an agreement could be reached, urging concessions on both sides.

preseason '69

Baseball Getting back to Normal

by Red Foley

*B*aseball finally got away from the bargaining table and back to the ballpark yesterday after the warring owners and the Players Association announced a compromise that returned the game to the fans. Word that the dispute had been settled was first published in yesterday's final edition of The News.

As in all agreements between management and labor, this contract, which was finally announced shortly after noon, has to be ratified by both sides. This is considered a mere formality, since Marvin Miller, executive director of the Association, immediately recommended that all players report to their respective training bases.

Players will now be eligible for pensions after four rather than five years of service. Retirement benefits were increased from $50 to $60 per month for each of the first 10 years of active service. The benefits for players with major league service from 11-20 years was also raised from $10 to $20 per month.

Players now can retire at age 45, with an actuarial adjustment from the benefits payable upon normal retirement at age 50. Life insurance coverage will be increased to $50,000 for each active player and $25,000 for each presently inactive player who qualifies for retirement.

Baseball commissioner Bowie Kuhn termed the agreement "fair to both players and clubs" and urged prompt approval of the contract that terminated a player strike that would have gone into effect on Saturday.

Miller was "happy," but not ecstatic. He said the defections by a minority of players, who spurned the boycott, hurt his bargaining power.

"The players held ranks remarkably well," he said. "You can't believe what pressure some of them were under. Nobody is being critical of the others, but facts are facts." ∎

DAILY NEWS

New York Mets manager Gil Hodges (left) and GM Johnny Murphy at the Mets' St. Petersburg training site.

preseason '69

Mets Raise Seaver to $35,000

by Dick Young

The Untouchables, *starring Tom Seaver and Jerry Koosman, was the name of the suspenseless drama unfolded here today. Seaver signed at $35,000, Kooz at $25,000, and both expressed supreme delight over their substantial raises. Seaver is 24, Koosman 25.*

"They were easy to sign," said Johnny Murphy, GM. "These are the two guys we call our untouchables, and they are worth the money." Untouchables refer to their untradability in talks with other clubs during the winter. Both pitched for the NL All-Stars.

Seaver won 16 last season: Koosman 19. If it doesn't add up that the guy with the three fewer wins is getting $10,000 more, the explanation is that Seaver has two years in the bigs, and Koosman one. Seaver got a 40% raise over his $25,000 of last year. Koosman started his rookie season as a $10,000 minimum man, got a merit raise to $15,000 near season's end, and now has jumped some 65% to $25G.

The financial graph is apparent. What Seaver gets one year, Kooz gets the next. It's a nice arrangement that both boys hope continues.

Infielder Al Weis also signed, and Murphy says Art Shamsky and Ken Boswell have agreed via phone. That leaves only four—Kranepool, Agee, Swoboda and J.C. Martin—on the outside . . . Murphy says Kranepool should be here tomorrow and is virtually signed. The other three haven't been heard from. ∎

DAILY NEWS Gene Kappock

Mets manager Gil Hodges (left) sports a smile. Who wouldn't with a threesome like (l to r) Jerry Koosman, Tom Seaver and Nolan Ryan on his pitching staff?

DAILY NEWS Dan Farrell

Gil Hodges

Hodges: He Turned Fans from Hahs to Hurrahs

by Dick Young

Which is the real Gil Hodges? Is it the ice-blooded tyrant depicted by Ken Harrelson, who played for Hodges in Washington and who says he couldn't wait to be traded away? Or is Gil Hodges the sainted Messiah, immaculate of habit, noble of character, and sent by the heavens to lead the Mets to their inescapable destiny.

It seems fair to say Gil Hodges is neither saint nor Satan. He has sinned. He has lost doubleheaders. He has left a pitcher in there too long. But Gil Hodges also has done miracles, transforming the Mets from baseball's biggest joke to baseball's biggest surprise. He has turned the spelling of The Amazins, with the sardonic capital-A, to amazing!—With a small, sincere a, and a genuine exclamation point. He has made the Amazin' Mets play major league ball.

There will always be personality clashes between managers and players. There will sometimes be Ken Harrelson cases. As long as baseball is a game played every day, there will be mistakes and impatience, and defeat, and anger. Even a pennant-winner loses 50 or more games a season. Only the fan in the stands is infallible.

"There is one thing the second-guesser does not take into consideration," said Gil Hodges. This came up during a discussion of managers' moves. "The man in the stands, the man in the pressbox, is not always on top of the situation."

"He knows an awful lot about baseball," said Jerry Koosman on the Mets bus in Chicago. Kooz was talking about Gil Hodges, without being asked. "He's always a step or two ahead. I've seen him do something, not a play ahead, but an inning ahead. He has a lot of baseball savvy."

"He has a lot of patience," said Bud Harrelson. ("Please don't confuse me with Ken Harrelson. I don't want to get blamed for that.") "That's the thing he has more than the others did, I guess, patience. He sticks with you longer, and that helps. You don't panic. You don't say, I have to get a hit today or my fanny will be on that bench."

Pitcher Don Cardwell has been around longer than the other Mets. He is more of Gil Hodges' generation. Ask him what has made the Mets so much better so much ahead of schedule and he says:

"I guess it's because Number 14 has climbed on a few rear ends. Watch him before a game. You'll see him wandering around behind the infield, or walking around the outfield, talking to a guy here and there. I think he's getting across the message to play a little more heads-up ball. They're human. They're gonna make some more mistakes. There will be letdowns, like what we're going through now. We just been playing dead. But he keeps after them to minimize the mistakes."

Tips on Managing

Treat every man on your team alike. Play no favorites. They are all here for the same purpose; to do what they can to win. Try to remember that. Also, try to remember that once you make rules for conduct for your ballclub, they apply to every man on the club. You will be tested. Managers always are. Be ready for it. Be firm, but be fair, and be it to the No. 25 man on your team, just as much as to the No. 1 man.

—Gil Hodges

Casey Stengel gives a few pointers to the Mets in the dugout at the St. Petersburg, Florida, training facility. Manager Gil Hodges (second from left) listens.

Spring Training '69

With the labor dispute resolved, the Mets quickly brought their players into the fold—with slugger Ron Swoboda and catcher J.C. Martin the last to sign.

With his numbers one and two pitchers already decided, Gil Hodges was left with the task of filling out his rotation with fireballer Nolan Ryan, rookie Gary Gentry and veteran Don Cardwell. But Hodges' decisions during the season were not his alone to make as Ryan and reliever Tug McGraw, among others, would have to report for military duty during the season.

While the Mets' pitching was expected to be strong, the hitting was not. However, when the Mets knocked the defending National League Champion Cardinals for 22 hits in a 16-6 spring training win in Florida, those in the stands sensed that something special might be in the making.

There was hope, but whether it was well founded was up for considerable debate.

Mets at 100%

Swoboda, Martin Complete Signings

by Dick Young

 **R**on Swoboda was dressing alone. The Mets had taken the field a half-hour earlier, and during that time he had been in the office wrangling a $27,000 contract out of Johnny Murphy, "Enough to cover the surtax," as Ron referred to the $2,000 goodwill raise.

spring training '69

When Swoboda came out of the room, J.C. Martin went in and soon the Mets were signed 100%.

Swoboda pulled on his cap, buttoned his No. 4 shirt, and reached into the top of his locker. There were two gloves there. He hesitated: "Which one should I take?"

"What difference does it make?" said a newsman.

Swoboda grinned broadly, and trotted through the door to the field. After the workout, the talk resumed about his contract, and about last season, and next.

"The thing I've got to do most," he said, "Is make it up with Gil. They tell me he's the kind of guy who doesn't hold a grudge. That's good."

They didn't get along last season. Hodges is a strong-willed man. Swoboda is a strong-willed child.

"I pulled a lot of things," said Swoboda. "The weren't real bad, but they weren't what Gil calls professional. That's what he wants of me, to be more pro."

Did Swoboda mean things like the game in Miami last spring? It was against the Orioles that he left the bench during the game to go to the john. He didn't tell anybody and the game went on without him.

"That was nothing," said Ron Swoboda. "There were other things during the season like throwing helmets and moping in the outfield, Gil doesn't care for that kind of stuff."

Players noted the difference between Swoboda and Tommie Agee. Agee would strike out and go to the field and make a diving catch. Swoboda would strike out and think about it all the way to right field, and suddenly there was a fly ball going over his thinking head.

"You've got to leave your hitting at the plate," Hodges told him more than once. Then, they would have words. ■

Mets Choose Sides for the 7 Jobs up for Grabs

March 4, 1969
by Dick Young

Job competition, in the shape of camp games, starts tomorrow for the Amazin' Mets. The emphasis, according to Gil Hodges, will be on finding a third baseman, a first baseman, starting pitchers Numbers 4 and 5, a lefty reliever and outfielders 4 and 5.

This translates into the fact that the Mets are set, or barely set, at shortstop, second, catcher, three starting pitchers, righty bullpen strength and regular outfield. That's progress.

Beating Yanks Has Lost Its Thrill

by Dick Young

**G**il Hodges feels the Mets are good enough and established enough in New York that they need no longer strive for the propaganda value of beating the Yankees in Florida. Therefore, Gary Gentry and Bob Hendley will pitch against the Yanks tonight, and the Ed Charles experiment goes into effect at first base.*

Time was when the Mets, under Casey Stengel, would bust a gut to beat the Yanks down here. It was like a college football coach trying to mousetrap Notre Dame; he could blow the rest of the games and still consider his season a huge success.

That was back when the Yankees were great and the Mets were laughable. Now they are equal. Both are highly mediocre.

"It certainly would be good to beat them," said Gil Hodges today, "but we stick to our pitching rotation regardless. That's why Koosman pitched yesterday and Seaver the day before. They came due that way."

The Yankees, by pitching lefty Fritz Peterson, afford Hodges the opportunity to start righty-swinger Ed Charles at first base. Hodges is playing mental gymnastics with a platoon of Charles and Ed Kranepool. Something, perhaps that, has had a salubrious effect upon Kranepool's energies of late.

"He's hustling and even opening his mouth on the bench and in the field," says Hodges, happy to discover that the No. 7 uniform is not being worn by an automaton.

A kid named Rod Gaspar, tall, stringy, and switch-hitting, could knock all the experimentation out of the ballpark. He has been the most impressive newcomer in camp. Check that; he has been the most impressive oldcomer in camp, too, with the possible exception of Cleon Jones.

Gaspar is pushing Ron Swoboda hard for the right field job. Yesterday, he pushed Ron over to left. There is a likelihood, Hodges admits, that opening a regular outfield spot for Gaspar would necessitate moving Cleon Jones to first base. "Anybody can play first base," says Hodges, who spent a lifetime there. ∎

Now Mets 'Dem Bombs, 16-6

March 15, 1969
by Dick Young

The Amazin' Mets, mopping up the other half of the 1968 World Series tandem, today mortified the NL champ Cardinals, 16-6, with 22 (count 'em, 22) hits that included homers by Amos Otis, Al Weis and Ken Singleton. Two days earlier, the Amazins humiliated the world champion Tigers, 12-0. Both games were played with the dead ball, and some arms to match.

The outcome of today's game was in suspense until the Mets batted in the top of the first. The top six batters hit safely and by the time the frame ended, the Mets had nine hits and a 7-0 head start.

Who's Gil Got on First? Meet Cleon

by Dick Young

Do the Mets have the guts to take their best ballplayer and move him to another position? Not only have, but will. The great experiment will start within the next few days, perhaps by Thursday: Cleon Jones at first base.

spring training '69

"I'm gonna try it soon," said Gil Hodges as he ran the Mets through today's open-date drill. "Maybe Thursday, maybe over the weekend. The kid is forcing us to make a move."

The kid is Rod Gaspar, camp phenom. He has played left, right and center and looked good at all down here. He has looked good with the bat, lefty and righty. He stings the ball, rarely strikes out. In 36 at-bats he has struck out once, and he is hitting .333. His nine RBIs are second only to Cleon's 13.

Nobody took the kid too seriously when he got here. You could tell by his uniform. You don't give No. 57 to somebody you take seriously. "I guess," he says, grinning, "I got the last uniform they had."

"Mind you, it's nothing definite," warns Hodges. "I just want to try Cleon there and see how it works."

DAILY NEWS John Duprey

Mets (l to r) Ron Taylor, Cleon Jones and Ken Boswell celebrate.

Says Cleon Jones: "It's worth a try, I played some first base in high school. I played everything there. It's like anything else, if you get used to it you like it." ■

Quartet's '67 Form Return Could Jell Mets

(This is from a series of letters from major league managers to baseball writer Red Foley.)

*D*ear Red:

Pitching and a few "ifs" could put the Mets into a contending position. Pitching is our strongest suit, but a return to 1967 form by Eddie Kranepool, Ron Swoboda, Bud Harrelson and Tommie Agee would do wonders for our chances in 1969. There's no doubt in my mind that with players such as Tom Seaver and Jerry Koosman, we can win the Eastern Division.

Our minor league department is high on youngsters like righthander Gary Gentry, Amos Otis and infielder Mike Jorgensen and if these kids come through we'll be that much ahead of the game.

We feel our pitching is a plus. Seaver and Koosman are a terrible pair for owners, although I'll admit that it remains to be seen if Jerry can put it back-to-back. Cal Koonce and Ron Taylor solidify our bullpen.

Nolan Ryan, Jim McAndrew, Don Cardwell, Al Jackson and Bob Hendley will all be in St. Pete trying for starting berths, too. Dan Frisella, Tug McGraw and rookie Barry Raziano are three others who just might win themselves pitching spot on this club.

Jerry Grote remains our No. 1 catcher. J.C. Martin and Duffy Dyer should scrap for the backup job in the department. At first base we figure right now to have two solid candidates: Kranepool, Jorgensen and perhaps Art Shamsky in reserve.

Ken Boswell and Bobby Heise figure to stage a dandy battle for the second base job. Harrelson, whose balky knee has been surgically repaired, should be our No. 1 shortstop.

Cleon Jones is our No. 1 outfielder. We feel he's just about ready to blossom into stardom. He does everything well, and to our way of thinking can be as good a player as he wants to be. Agee and Swoboda will be out there, with Shamsky and 22-year-old Rod Gaspar also bidding for outfield berths.

In my opinion, Swoboda has the ability to be a fine hitter. He needs confidence, however. To me, that's the difference between Ron and possible stardom.

I won't give up on Agee, either. Tommie has fine potential and he certainly hasn't given up on himself.

I know the question of my health still has some people wondering about Gil Hodges' immediate future as Mets' manager. Well, all I can say is that I've never felt better and the doctors, who are pleased with my progress, assure me I can look forward to managing the Mets this season.

And believe me that's just what I'm going to do.

Sincerely,
Gil Hodges ■

spring training '69

Mets Gas Past Twins, 12-4

by Dick Young

*O*utstanding in today's final exhibition action, as the Amazin' Mets walloped the Twins, 12-4, in seven innings, then led them again, 5-1, in a plane-catching 4 1/2 frames, were Ed Charles, Jerry Grote, Cleon Jones, all of whom hit long homers; J.C. Martin, who poled a rocketing triple; and Fred Cavet.

The New Orleans Commission lured the Mets and Twins here for the Easter weekend to create a major league impression, just in case some depressed franchise should be looking around for a new home in, say, three or four years.

There were to have been single games yesterday and today. Yesterday it poured, so the unique exhibition doubleheader was scheduled. The New Orleans promotors asked for it. Managers Gil Hodges and Billy Martin consented because their pitchers needed work. But both teams had planes to make. They would play, they agreed, two seven-inning games, starting at noon and ending at 4 p.m. regardless.

It was into a wooded area that Grote and Cleon Jones sent the Minny outfielders running for their inside-the-park homers. Ed Charles lost one in the trees beyond the left end of the horseshoe. Two throwing efforts by Leo Cardenas set up the shots by Charles and Grote and led to a seven-run third in the opener.

The second game was a 1-1 tie till the Mets scored three on a double by Ed Kranepool, Martin's long triple and a popfly homer by Bud Harrelson. Bud's beaut, about 250 feet, wouldn't have been a homer in the Polo Grounds.

The Mets finished their spring with a record of 14-10 and that 4/5th of a win they had when curfew rung and Tug McGraw was left standing out there on the lower mound with his mouth open. ∎

Ron Swoboda takes batting practice, which paid off as spring training came to an end.

spring training '69

A Whiz Computer's Unsentimental Forecast

by Bud Goode

ho will win the AL and NL pennants this year? Who were the best clutch teams in 1968? What are the chances of scoring in a game if the bases are loaded and no one is out? What determines the real difference between ballclubs?

The answers to these, and the million and one other baseball questions under the sun, were usually determined by baseball pundits and crystal ball gazers who depended on hunches, guesswork and a loose smattering of statistics. With the advent of computerized research, the hit-or-miss method of predicting is a thing of the past, as extinct as the dinosaur.

The computer has taken over. It knows no sentiment, favoritism or prejudice and uses only the cold facts and figures fed into it to arrive at impersonal decisions and predictions.

And there's no guesswork about it!

Now, as for the answers to the questions in the first paragraph: Detroit and St. Louis figure to repeat as champs . . . The computer rated Cincinnati and Detroit as the best clutch-hitting teams in 1968 . . . The seventh inning isn't really a "lucky inning" at all . . . The first and the third innings are the frames in which most runs are scored.

In predicting the team standings, millions of statistics go into the final figure—which we call the Strength Ratio. That's the figure that indicates where the team will finish in the standings. The computer digests its millions of facts to estimate the number of runs a team will score, and the number of runs its opposition will score against it.

This ratio of runs to opponent's runs is a perfect measure of a club's offensive-defensive ability because it includes batting, pitching and fielding. And it also includes clutch factors, something never attempted before on a statistical basis.

Here's what the computer has to say about the contenders.

NL East

St. Louis is still the class of the NL. The Cards are strong at every position, and key factors are that they actually strengthened themselves with the acquisition of Joe Torre from the Braves and Vada Pinson from Cincy. They rate as the top defensive club in baseball.

Slugging Pittsburgh is as strong offensively as St. Louis, but the Pirates are still unable to come up with some pitching to match their power.

Another strong club is Chicago, but the computer says the Cubs will give up as many runs as they score.

Strange as it seems, the computer picks the New York Mets as the "dark horse" in the East. Defensively, the Mets are second only to the Cards. They have some excellent young hurlers. However, the Mets need to score 100 more runs to challenge. The computer pinpoints their inability to win close games as a major factor in their 9th-place finish last year.

spring training '69

DAILY NEWS

Tom Seaver

Picking Seaver: Greatest Hat Trick of All Time

by Dick Young

Dennis Ribant's fastball sailed on Tom Seaver and struck him hard on the right elbow. "There goes the franchise," somebody in the pressbox said. Newsmen rushed down to the Forbes Field visiting clubhouse. Inside, Gus Mauch was applying an icepack to the area. Outside stood a few interested people, including Nancy Seaver. A newsman came out of the Mets clubhouse and smiled at her. She shook her head, and every bobbed blonde hair remained in place. "The right arm," she protested. "Why couldn't it have hit him on the head?"

"That's my loving wife," says Tom Seaver when the frightening day in 1967 is recalled. "She's a very good needler. She keeps me in touch with reality."

"He's the greatest guy in the world," says Bud Harrelson. Next to a wife, nobody knows a ballplayer better than his roomie. On the road, Bud Harrelson rooms with Tom Seaver. "He doesn't walk around with his head in the clouds and say I'm the greatest pitcher in the National League," says Bud Harrelson. "He might well be."

Harry Walker, baseball scientist, takes moving pictures of every phase of the game and makes slides from them to teach classic form at all positions. For his discourses on pitching, Harry Walker uses pictures of Tom Seaver.

Says Rube Walker, Mets pitching coach: "Seaver has great control of himself, as well as his pitches. Nothing upsets him very much."

"He has a reliability quality," says Gil Hodges. "You know that every time he comes due he'll be out there. You can mark it on the calendar. I rate him with Don Drysdale."

There is no higher praise from Gil Hodges than that you be mentioned in the same breath with Don Drysdale. Through their time together on the Dodgers, and still, Gil Hodges loved Don Drysdale as much as any man loves another.

Tom Seaver was a sophomore at USC when the Los Angeles Dodgers drafted him in June of 1965. They did not offer him enough money to give up school, so Tom Seaver declined to sign. The following January the Braves took a shot at him. They said $50,000.

Tom Seaver liked the sound of that. He signed. The baseball commissioner's office discovered a technical violation in the signing and declared Tom Seaver a free agent. It was ruled that, excluding the Braves, any club wishing to match the original $50,000 bonus could qualify for the Tom Seaver lottery.

Three responded—the Phillies, Indians and Mets. Their names were put in a hat. The commissioner reached in and pulled out the magic slip. Of all William D. Eckert's accomplishments while serving as baseball commissioner, none will be so long remembered as the scouting job he did that day for the Mets.

In justice to the Mets' front office, however, it should be reflected upon that they were one of only four clubs willing to risk $50,000 on an untried college kid. Sixteen big league clubs did not respond.

It did not take long for Tom Seaver to become the bargain of the year. He was proclaimed the NL's outstanding rookie in 1967. His record was 16 and 13. In 1968, he was 16 and 12, and at one stage ripped off 22 straight zips.

Tips on Pitching

The biggest thing a young pitcher should do is **get his body to absorb** part of the strain of pitching. **Make the back, the** hips, the thighs carry some **of the work, not just** the arm. It came natural to **me, but it can be** learned. It will make your **arm last longer.**

—Tom Seaver

N. Y. Mets right-hander Nolan Ryan works on his delivery under supervision of Mets coaches Wes Stock (left) and Rube Walker.

April '69

They seemed like the same old Mets on Opening Day. The Mets outhit the Expos 15-12 and scored four runs in the ninth inning, but still came up short with an opening day loss, 11-10. This was their eighth straight opening day loss—this time to an expansion club.

As the Mets' young guns on the mound struggled with soreness and injury, Gil Hodges turned to veteran Don Cardwell to lead them out of their slump. That was just the beginning, as Gil shook things up by benching Tommie Agee and training camp-phenom rookie Rod Gaspar.

The shake-up worked. The Mets righted their floundering vessel to thump the Cardinals. The Mets were even so bold as to step above the defending NL champs in the divisional standings.

While the Cards dropped, the Cubs staked out their turf at the top of the NL East, under the guidance of the colorful Leo Durocher.

But the Mets were now moving in a new direction—up. They finished April in third place and only three games below .500. Lofty heights at that time for the Amazin' Mets.

Expos Spoil Met Opener

by Norm Miller

O pening Day 1969 for the Mets was historic, hysterical and downright embarrassing. It wasn't bad enough that they blew a season opener for the eighth straight year of their existence yesterday at Shea. To blow it 11-10 to the expansionist Montreal Expos, a grab-bag team resembling the Mets of yesteryear, was something else.

At that, the Mets gave the 44,541 first-day showups a whooping good time for their money in this first international major league game ever played. They rallied for four runs in the ninth, three coming on a pinch homer by rookie catcher Duffy Dyer, and put runners on first and second before Expo reliever Carroll Sembers fanned Rod Gaspar to end the three-hour 35-minute duel on a beautiful afternoon.

While the game had its elements of excitement for the fans, the defeat might have been summed up in Gil Hodges' most proper French, "Mon Dieu, c'etait terrible!"

It was a mish-mash in which Tom Seaver was lifted with a 6-4 lead after throwing 105 pitches in five innings; Met relievers botched the job, the Expos pulling away with four runs in the eighth off Al Jackson and Ron Taylor; and Met hitters almost pulled the game out with the four runs in the ninth.

Dyer, a 24-year-old rookie catcher who rates behind Jerry Grote and J.C. Martin, was one of three players who stroked his maiden major league homer in this game. Others were hit by Expos, the first by relief pitcher Dan McGinn, a Notre Dame grad, the second a three-run blast by third baseman Jose Laboy that pulled Montreal away by 11-6 in the eighth. Rusty Staub had homered to start that frame. ■

Bill Shea presents Mets' manager Gil Hodges with a good luck wreath before the season opener at Shea Stadium.

Shea Scene: There's Life in the Old Game Yet

April 9, 1969
by Dick Young

There were 44,541 people watching baseball die at Shea Stadium yesterday. They screamed, sang, yelled, whistled, stood and waved banners. No respect, these moderns.

It is still the national pastime, in a sporting sense, and all the fashionable cynicism, the absurd surveys, the smug derision, and the fumbling by the groping Lords of Baseball, hadn't changed that.

Football, pro football, has made substantial progress. Hockey and basketball are picking up. Golf has come a long way. Boxing is coming back from the tomb where television deposited it. But it's still King Baseball, monarch of the democratic world of sports.

All that is needed to remind you of this is a sunny spring afternoon, a late Easter week so dad can bring out the kids, a fairly good attraction, and baseball is right back on top.

Mets Were Playing a Patsy

Opening Day at Shea had a better than fair attraction. The New Breed had their beloved Mets, the improved beloved Mets, and the almost-guaranteed assurance that they were playing a worse team. There also was a bit of international spice. For the very first time, Canada had a club in the bigs. The red and white Maple Leaf, as well as the Stars and Stripes, brightened the scene.

The fellow sitting behind the red-leafed banner near the dugout, the one with the little hair and much spirit, was Jean Drapeau, mayor of Montreal. Drapeau means flag, and Johnny Flag is what his English-speaking constituents call him.

"Magnifique," said the mayor of Montreal, as the Expos grabbed a two-run lead in the first. Soon, hizzoneur was to learn what Bob Wagner and John Lindsay had learned before him. A lead can vanish quickly with an expansion club. It can vanish with a seven-year old expansion club.

Mons. Drapeau learned another valuable lesson, a vignette of life in New York. He was to throw out the first ball. About an hour before the ceremony, a man from the Mets walked up to him, held out a shiny new baseball, and said: "Mr. Mayor, this is the ball you will use. Please put it in your pocket so you will be sure to have it."

"Certainment," said Mons. Drapeau.

The mayor then made the rounds, lunch in the director's room, shaking hands in the Diamond Club, visiting the players in the dugouts. Lo, the big moment approached. Arthur Richman, who worries about such things, sidled up to Mons. Drapeau.

Mayor Left Ball in Dugout

"Mr. Mayor, do you have the baseball?"

"It is all right," said the mayor. "I place it in the dugout."

"You what?" said Arthur Richman.

"It is all right," said the mayor. "I put it on the seat at this end of the Montreal dugout. You will find it there."

The man ran across the field and into the dugout. He looked where he had been told, and saw what he had expected to see. Nothing. He went back to the mayor. "It is gone," he said. "Somebody took it. I will get you another. Please put this one in your pocket."

"Who would take it?" said the puzzled mayor of Montreal.

1969 Mets Starting Lineup

Tommy Agee, cf
Rod Gaspar, rf
Ken Boswell, 2b
Cleon Jones, lf
Ed Charles, 3b
Ed Kranepool, 1b
Jerry Grote, c
Bud Harrelson, ss
Tom Seaver, p

Mets Get First Win as Tug Stops Expos

by Norm Miller

Tug McGraw—who in 1965 became the first Met pitcher ever to beat the great Sandy Koufax—yesterday gained the distinction of being the first major leaguer ever to subdue the Montreal Expos. McGraw did it with 6 1/3 fine innings of relief pitching that earned the Mets their first win of the new season, 9-5, at Shea.

In achieving his first win as a Met since 1966, McGraw pitched six shutout frames in relief of Jim McAndrew before he ran out of gas in the eighth and had to be bailed out by Nolan Ryan. Ryan was tagged for Rusty Staub's second homer in as many days before completing the save.

For the second straight day at Shea, it was a game in which one team or the other scored in eight of the nine innings. Among the Mets' 12 hits was a homer by Ken Boswell. Cleon Jones, Ed Kranepool and Jerry Grote each drove in a pair of runs before the crowd of 13,827.

McGraw has had a checkered career since he first came up to the Mets as a 20-year-old Rookie in 1965. One of his two wins that season was a triumph over Koufax.

The following season, he again won two games, the last during August, before his development was slowed by a hitch in the Marines, and a stretch of elbow and shoulder trouble. He had an 0-3 record with the Mets in '67 and spent all last year on the Jacksonville, Illinois farm.

McGraw gave the Mets their first good pitching job of the new season as he worked his way out of a bases-loaded, no-out jam in the second, when the Expos threatened to wipe out an early 4-0 Mets lead. ■

DAILY NEWS John Duprey

Tug McGraw delivers from the mound. He became the first pitcher to defeat the Montreal Expos.

Agee Reborn

Two Mighty Home Runs Whip Expos, 2-4

by Larry Fox

Truly a new era, at least for the day, at Shea Stadium—Gary Gentry, pitching and winning his first major league ball game; Tommie Agee hitting two home runs in one game for the first time in his pro career, including an unprecedented smash into the upper deck in left; and the Mets declining to give it all away in the ninth inning when they had a perfect chance to blow yesterday's 4-2 victory over the Expos.

Agee's bat explosion was the most heart-warming. The husky centerfielder had suffered through a dismal introductory season after he joined the Mets last year. He batted only .217 and it took a late batting spurt to get that high.

And Ron Swoboda, who holds the Met record for long homers with a smash over the second fence in left his rookie year, said: "That one today would have gone over the third fence and hit the bus in the parking lot if it hadn't hit the seats."

"This meant a lot to me," Agee said of his performance as he nodded toward Hodges' office. "Not many managers would have had enough faith to go with me after the year I had." ■

DAILY NEWS Dan Farrell

N. Y. Mets Tommie Agee (left) and Jerry Koosman

April '69

Cards Rap Seaver

Gibson 3-hitter sweeps Mets, 3-1

by Larry Fox

The rulemakers didn't go far enough in their off-season efforts to help the hitters, the Mets have learned. They forgot to outlaw Bob Gibson. Gibson completed the Cardinal's Shea sweep by pitching a three-hitter for a 3-1 victory, the seventh straight time he has beaten the Mets over three seasons.

Gibson's lifetime record is now 22-3 against the New Yorkers, which puts him one up on Juan Maichal (21-2) and one down on Don Drysdale (23-6) among active Met killers. He beat them four in a row last season. The last time he lost to them was May 14, 1967.

A 22-game winner in 1968, Gibson went nine on Opening Day but was not involved in the decision as the Pirates beat the Cards, 6-2, in 14.

Yesterday's decision marked the third straight loss by the Mets and the third straight victory for the defending NL champions, who had dropped their first three at home.

The Cardinals won it in the very first inning against Tom Seaver, who has had a difficult start again this year.

Lou Brock led off with a first-pitch double to right-center and took third on Curt Flood's single to deep short on which Bud Harrelson made a good stop in the hole. Brock held as Flood took second on a wild pitch and then he scored and Flood moved to third on another wild pitch by the young right-hander. Tim McCarver's sacrifice fly delivered Flood.

The Mets didn't get a hit until Ed Kranepool led off the fifth with a double. He scored on Harrelson's single. ■

National League Eastern Division

As of April 14

Team	Wins	Losses	Percentage	Games Back
Pittsburgh	5	1	.833	—
Chicago	4	2	.667	1
Montreal	3	3	.500	2
St. Louis	3	3	.500	2
METS	2	4	.333	3
Philadelphia	1	5	.167	4

Bucs' Moose Untouchable

by Dick Young

The untouchable young Met pitchers gave another unspeakable performance tonight. Jerry Koosman was knocked out in three, Nolan Ryan took a short but traumatic massaging, and the Bucs piled it up, 11-3, on 15 hits.

In the eyes of the 7,666 Pitt fans, their boy Bob Moose was the genuine untouchable. He whiffed 11, and had only one hard time, in the fourth. It was then that the Mets got back into the game, briefly.

They went into the frame trailing 5-1. Kooz had been rocked for four in the first, Jose Pagan's triple being the boomingest of five Buc hits in the bat-around.

Suddenly, the Mets got in on the extra-base picnic. Ken Boswell opened the fourth with a triple down the right-center slot, Jones scratched a single in front of the plate, then both men came in on Ed Kranepool's drive down the triple lane. It was now 5-3 with Kranepool on third and none down. Anything at all would deliver him and make it a one-run ball game.

The Mets didn't get anything at all. A weak grounder by Amos Otis, a K by Martin, another bouncer by Harrelson and Kranepool died on third. If there were any doubts that the Mets were done, they dissipated quickly. The Bucs batted around again, knocking out Ryan. ■

Kids Can't Do It, So Mets Turn to Cardwell

April 18, 1969
by Dick Young

They're turning to Pops Cardwell tonight for help. The kids have had their fun, and all the talk about youth and verve and improvement is delightful dreams stuff but when the Mets are in trouble they turn to the old man for help, and right now the Mets are in trouble. They have lost five of their last six.

Their great young arms are falling down on the job. Jerry Koosman and Nolan Ryan last night were belted by the Bucs, who ran around the bases in an 11-3 shallumping. There were 15 hits, some quite long.

Don Cardwell will try to cool off the Bucs tonight. Don Cardwell is old. You can tell he is old. He wears crew-cut hair. He also knows how to pitch. He pitched the only good game the Mets have had pitched for them to date. He gave up a run. That is one more than the Mets made that day against the Cardinals, so Don Cardwell lost his six-hitter.

Don Cardwell, 33, is the only Met to pitch nine innings in a ball game this year. He will try it again tonight. He will be facing the Pitt A-team. This is the one with Willie Stargell. Last night Stargell didn't play. That is what is frightening to the Mets.

Hodges Shaking Up Shook-Up Mets

by Dick Young

*T*he untouchable Mets not only are being touched, they are being gruffly shaken. Manager Gil Hodges is benching Tommie Agee and Rod Gaspar for tonight's set-opener with St. Louis, and is moving Amos Otis from third base to center field.

To fill in the gaps, Kevin Collins will get a shot at third base and Ron Swoboda will be back at his old stand in right, the spot he was beaten out of in Florida by the phenom conduct of Rod Gaspar. Till now, Swoboda has been leftfielding only against lefty pitching.

To that extent, the platoon goes out the window. Swoboda faces Bob Gibson tonight, and there are few pitchers more righthanded than Hoot Gibson. ■

DAILY NEWS Dan Farrell

Mets manager Gil Hodges

Mets Throttle Cards

April 21, 1969
by Dick Young

Red Schoendienst, a sad seer, said in New York recently, after his Cardinals had swept the Mets in three games: "They're a good ballclub. They will be tough to beat." Today, the Mets were too tough to beat. They blasted the champs, 11-3, on the solid ribby stickwork of the bottom batting order men—Ed Kranepool, Ron Swoboda, Jerry Grote and Kevin Collins—to take the curtailed two-set.

The shocked Birds are 0-and-7 at home, and behind the Mets in the Eastern sector.

Cubs May Be in Trouble

Lead Majors in Ex-Mets

by Larry Fox

asey Stengel said it: *"If I can get enough of my guys on those other teams and ruin them, too, then maybe we'll have a chance to win a pennant."* Which means the first-place Cubs, who came into Shea to open a four-game series against the Mets last night, are in trouble.

Not the trouble of a mere half-game lead over the Pirates or a four-game losing streak, but deeper difficulties. With the addition of Dick Selma via a late Thursday night trade, for a total of three, the Cubs now lead both major leagues in ex-Mets.

San Diego freed itself of that distinction by that trade and now is tied with Montreal in second place. The Padres' ex-Mets are Chris Cannizzaro and Larry Stahl. The Expos roster has Don Shaw and Don Bosch.

All told, 19 former Shea residents are still in the majors, and when Selma joins the Cubs he will be reunited with Jim (an original) Hickman and Charlie Smith.

The Cubs are wasting no time putting Selma to work. He's scheduled to pitch his first game for them in tomorrow's doubleheader at Shea. It would be nice if Leo Durocher gave Hickman and Smith a start in the same game, just for old time's sake. ■

National League Eastern Division

As of April 26

Team	Wins	Losses	Percentage	Games Back
Chicago	11	5	.688	—
Pittsburgh	10	5	.667	1/2
METS	6	8	.429	4
Montreal	6	9	.400	4 1/2
St. Louis	6	9	.400	4 1/2
Philadelphia	5	8	.385	4 1/2

Cubs Beat Mets

Kessinger homers in the third inning

by Larry Fox

The division-leading Cubs attempted to break a four-game losing streak last night when they sent Ferguson Jenkins against the Mets' Tom Seaver before 18,548 at Shea Stadium and Jenkins helped himself with a fifth-inning home run.

The Cubs won, 3-1.

The most unlikely of candidates put the Cubs ahead with a home run in the third inning. Two men were out when shortstop Don Kessinger's hit his first homer of the season, only the third of a major league career that began in 1965 and his first as a left-hander. It wasn't until last year that the .239 lifetime batter turned to switch-hitting.

The Cubs added another run in the fourth, again on a two-strike home run off Seaver. This time it was Ron Santo, hitting a 1-2 pitch over the fence in left, his fourth of the season.

The Mets threatened in the fourth when Cleon Jones (extending his consecutive game hitting streak to eight) and Ed Kranepool, led off with singles. Ron Swoboda sacrificed, but Jerry Grote popped to short. Kevin Collins was purposely walked and Seaver grounded out. ∎

Mets Down, 8-6; Up 3-0 on Jones Home Run

April 28, 1969
by Red Foley

On a day when the nation pushed its clocks ahead, the Mets, showing a marvelous sense of timing, yesterday split a Shea twinner with the Cubs in which they gave 37,437 customers a look at the dismal past and then a peek into the glorious future.

Cleon Jones, who spans both eras, introduced the faithful to their promised land when he busted a two-on homer in the ninth for the 3-0 triumph that followed the four-run final frame giveaway that blew the 8-6 opener.

Jones' fifth hit of the long matinee, the one that hoisted his league-leading average to .443, came on a 1-0 delivery by luckless lefty Rich Nye. Rod Gaspar and Ken Boswell, on via gifts of one kind or another, preceded cloutin' Cleon across to fracture what had been a scoreless pitching duel.

Among the more ecstatic Mets to mob Jones at the plate was Tug McGraw. The lefty, who did a snazzy job of rescuing starter Jim McAndrew in the sixth, finally found a home—in the Mets' bullpen. And this time city zoning laws won't prevent it. You may remember that Tug originally wanted to park his two-room trailer at Shea, but the statutes prohibited it.

Durocher, Baseball's "Liberace" without Candelabra

by Larry Fox

They may never call him Mr. Baseball but that's okay because they should probably call him Mr. Show Business. That's what all of it is to Leo Durocher—show business.

The Cubs were on a four-game losing streak as they prepared to open the weekend series here with the Mets. But was Leo Durocher worried? Not on your manicure. He was sitting there in the manager's room of the Cubs' Shea Stadium clubhouse telling the boys about his appearance on the Dean Martin show.

"When was that filmed?" someone asked.

"Back in February," said the Lip, who used to threaten to quit the National Pastime about every other year with the boast that he could be making twice as much in show business.

"He's so funny!" Leo says of pal Dean. "When we finished the show, he and the producer and his wife were guests of mine in Acapulco for about 10 days. I rent this house down there. So one day Dean says, 'I've been your guest long enough. Today, we're goin' out.'"

Now Leo doesn't have to threaten to quit baseball and go into show business.

The contract he signed with the Cubs this year is said to be substantially above the 65 thousand he made in 1968. And John Holland, the Cub GM, said at the time the only reason there is a contract at all is that baseball law required it.

"Leo knows he can manage the Cubs as long as he wants to," Holland said.

It beats getting fired twice a week by Larry MacPhail. ■

Chicago Cubs manager Leo Durocher.

DAILY NEWS Charles Hoff

Downpour Helps Hodges Forget Swoboda Miscues

by Red Foley

Gil Hodges uttered no complaint when the pitter-patter of yesterday's April shower, the kind that brings May flowers and twi-night doubleheaders, took precedence over the pitter-patter of Ron Swoboda's runaway feet.

In fact, the day-long downpour, which turned Shea into a hazy bog, and caused early postponement of the Mets-Phillies matinee, is probably regarded as a help rather than a hindrance.

For one thing it gave Hodges additional time to court the brand of amnesia that might help him forget Monday night's 11-inning loss and Swoboda's singularly unforgettable performance in same.

Swoboda banged two of the five hits the Mets collected, knocked in their lone run and contributed one of his famous routinely sensational self-defense catches. But you ain't heard of it yet.

He had just knocked in the go-ahead run and was on first with Ed Charles on third. Then Swoboda stalled the Mets' offense by thinking.

With Ed Kranepool at bat, Swoboda suddenly broke for second. No one, least of all Hodges, ordered it, and the move amazed all but Philly catcher Mike Ryan. He took one squint at Charles, who was mesmerized at third, and promptly whistled the peg to shortstop Don Money that nailed the by-now unsure Swoboda a mile-and-a-half from second base. ■

DAILY NEWS Gene Kappock

Mets manager Gil Hodges (left) has had more than a few chats with Ron Swoboda.

Kranepool's 2 Carry Mets to 2-0 Win

Kooz' Arm Fails

by Dick Young

 **Y**ou want the good news first? Ed Kranepool cracked his first two circuits of the year today to become the homeringest Met on record with 53, and to give the Mets a 2-0 victory over the Expos in their first game in Canada.

The bad news is Jerry Koosman's arm. It's sore again. He was buzzing along nicely in the fifth, working on a two-hitter when "it felt like a rubber-band stretching."

With only two outs needed to become eligible for a victory, a pitcher usually will try to luck it through.

"I couldn't," said Kooz later. "I felt like I couldn't lift my arm."

He seemed worried as he said it. Then, he smiled, "Now, I feel fine." He lifted his left arm overhead. "I feel I could go right out and pitch."

Nolan Ryan got the hurry call when Kooz' arm went rubbery. He was given the time needed to get ready, amidst bilingual catcalls of the 8,577 nippy-nosed fans. The announcer explained in French and English that the rules permit this when a pitcher is injured. The audience booed its understanding. ■

National League Eastern Division

As of April 30

Team	Wins	Losses	Percentage	Games Back
Chicago	16	6	.727	—
Pittsburgh	12	7	.722	1/2
METS	6	8	.429	4
Montreal	6	9	.400	4 1/2
St. Louis	6	9	.400	4 1/2
Philadelphia	5	8	.385	4 1/2

DAILY NEWS Gene Kappock

Jerry Koosman

They Couldn't Keep Kooz' Arm Down on the Farm

by Dick Young

W hen Jerry Koosman was a kid, he and his two brothers played 500 on the Koosman farm. As anyone from Appleton, Minnesota, knows, 500 is played with a bat and a ball.

"One guy hits the ball," Jerry Koosman explains patiently to the city kids, "and if you catch it on the fly you get 100 points. Catch it on the first bounce, you get 75. On two bounces, 50, and on three bounces 25. A roller is good for 15. The first guy to get 500 points gets up to hit."

Jerry Koosman did not play a game of baseball till he was 16. "Where do you get nine kids on one side when you live on a farm 11 miles north of Appleton?"

One Sunday, it was decided by Orville Koosman that his younger brother was ready to go to Appleton to play semi-pro ball. From there, things began to happen to Jerry Koosman. He started in the outfield, switched to pitching, and then there was the day he was working the big game, Appleton against Dumont. Jerry Koosman struck out the first 21 batters and walked majestically to the water bucket at the end of the seventh. A smallish man came over and introduced himself as a scout for the Giants.

"You're doing swell, kid," Koosman remembers him saying, "but you could throw even harder if you opened up a little more." The man talked about stepping here, instead of there, and when Jerry Koosman went out for the eighth he tried it. Koosman remembers walking two, hitting another, being clipped for a single, and eventually getting the side out after a couple of runs.

In the ninth, the first batter flied out to the fence, and Jerry Koosman decided to go back to his unprofessional way of pitching. He struck out the last two men.

Jerry Koosman says he never saw that man again, but other scouts started to show up, looking for that big left-handed farm boy who struck out 23.

As a rookie last season, Jerry Koosman won 19 games, a club record. He was nipped by Johnny Bench, Cincy catcher, in the Rookie of the Year voting. Kooz fired seven shutouts, matching something Grover Cleveland Alexander had done as a rookie in 1911. Irving M. Young also did it in 1905, but it sounds better to be compared to the great Alexander.

That quickly, Jerry Koosman has become Koufax to Tom Seaver's Drysdale. That may seem a bit presumptuous, even in this day of instant greatness. Gil Hodges, basically guarded, thinks not. "To us, Seaver and Koosman are Drysdale and Koufax," says the manager of the Mets. "I don't think Drysdale and Koufax, as good as they were, could be any more important to the Dodgers than these two are to the Mets."

Koosman is a cool cat. He reminds you of Warren Spahn in his approach to a game. Spahn would play pepper and generally horse around before taking his warm-up pitches. Most starting pitchers are uptight before a game. They are miles away, eyes glazed, thinking of how they are going to pitch to Willie Mays or Henry Aaron or Al Kaline. Jerry Koosman sits on the bench and jokes with newsmen and teammates and if somebody doesn't tell him it's time to warm up, he just might forget it.

This does not mean Jerry Koosman doesn't know the meaning of fear. He felt fear to the point of panic this spring, when his shoulder went sore for the first time in his life. It happened in camp and it happened again early in the season, at Montreal. It turned out to be nothing chronic, but there was no way to know that at the time.

"When it happens, you say to yourself, is this it? Is my whole life going down the drain now, after all my dreams?" reveals Koosman.

Tips on Pitching

Don't throw a curveball before you're 16. I didn't. If you are a father, don't let your boy do it. When you're young the bones in the arms are not strong enough. They are developing. Chips may break off in the elbow if you try to throw curves too soon. Doctors have told me that. You'll hurt your chances of pitching pro ball.

—Jerry Koosman

N. Y. Mets Ed Kranepool (7) and Ron Swoboda (4) greet Ed
Charles at home plate.

April showers bring May flowers. After being showered with abuse in the first month of the season, the Mets flowered in a series against the first-place Cubs. As pitchers Tom Seaver and Bill Hands traded beanballs, the Mets took two games away from the Cubs to climb even closer to the .500 mark. They would flirt with .500 all month, reaching the lofty plateau on May 21 with Tom Seaver's three-hit win over the Atlanta Braves. But the Mets wouldn't rest on that plateau. They were audacious enough to aim for the top of the NL East heap.

A week earlier, the Braves had been the Mets' victim in a 9-1 win as the Amazins scored eight runs in one inning after being no-hit for six innings by the Braves.

The Mets' pitching staff was coming back around as well. After weeks of inactivity, Jerry Koosman reestablished himself as an ace with a club-record 15 strikeouts against the expansion Padres.

The Mets couldn't entirely shake off their losing ways, as a slump late in the month left them four games under .500 and nine games behind Durocher's Cubs.

Cubs Chase Mets' Gentry, 6-4

by Dick Young

Gary Gentry, after two wins, today became a full-fledged Met. He lost for the first time in the bigs. The rookie fast-baller was doing just great until the fourth, when homers by Ron Santo and Al Spangler ripped him for four runs and led to the Cubs' 6-4 victory.

Tommie Agee, rested for two weeks, came back to work brimming with vitality. He banged four hits, including a shot onto the artificial green in center field. This is the Astroturf spread across the wide section of block-out seats. It is manufactured by Monsanto, and when Ron Santo put one deep up on the blanket in the fourth, somebody said that Ron Santo hit the Monsanto. Somebody is always saying little things like that.

Ron Santo did it to open the fourth and break up the zipmatch between Gentry and Ken Holtzman. There followed a single by ageless Ernie Banks, a walk to Randy Hundley and then a shot into the right bleachers by Al Spangler.

This cued Gil Hodges that Gary Gentry might not have it today because Al Spangler, in his 10 years of major league ball, has averaged 1.6 homers a year. He now has .6 to go for this season. ∎

DAILY NEWS Bill Meurer

N. Y. Mets pitcher Gary Gentry (left) and third baseman Amos Otis, two of the new Met faces of 1969, pay a call on Mrs. Payson at Shea Stadium.

Mets Pull Rocks, Ryan a Muscle in 3-2 Loss to Cubs

by Dick Young

Gil Hodges spent much of the afternoon telling the umpires they don't know what they're doing, and the umpires spent the rest of it thinking that Gil's players don't know too much about the game, either. The umpires, off the evidence, had much on their side as the Mets first lost Nolan Ryan for some time, then lost the 3-2 ballgame to the division-leading Cubs.

J.C. Martin and Ron Swoboda smashed early homers off Fergy Jenkins, and from there things went steadily downhill for the Mets. Nolan Ryan, given this 2-0 lead by the third, nursed it into the seventh, then threw himself out of the game with two gasp-provoking pegs.

The first came with men on first and second

and none down. Al Spangler dropped a bunt, and Ryan had an easy play at third. He heaved it, instead, to Cleon Jones in left. One man came in and the others wound up on second and third—and nobody out.

Mets pitcher Nolan Ryan.

Hodges came to the mound to tell Ryan he was going to let him work out his destiny. The appreciative youngster whiffed pinch-swinger Willie Smith—and then came the second gasp-making peg. Ryan blew a second-strike past pinch-swinger Manny Jiminez that had so much on it, the crowd of 23,228 went oooh—so did Ryan. He had pulled his right groin.

That was nothing compared to what the other Mets pulled. Cal Koonce got out of that inning still leading, 2-1. Then the bottom fell out.

Here, Ron Santo drove to right-center, Ron Gaspar, just moved over to right in a defensive switch, showed the risky abandon of youth. He tried to make a shoestring catch. Had he played it safe, the Cubs would have had men on first and second with one down.

Instead, the ball skipped by for a triple and the score was knotted. Koonce then issued two walks, on purpose, Al Jackson came in with the bags full to fan pinch-swinger Gene Oliver for the Big second out. But Ron Taylor walked pinch-looker Dolfo Phillips midst the righty-lefty switches, and there went the tough ballgame. ∎

Seaver, McGraw Stall Cub 'Flag' Bid, 3-2, 3-2

by Dick Young

his is something the Harris Poll will find hard to believe: With the Cubs fighting for the pennant in the first week of May, 40,484 fans today packed Wrigley Field to the beams for two baseball games. The Mets took them 3-2 and 3-2. That's something everybody will find hard to believe.

Also hard to believe was the sight of Ron Swoboda legging it all the way from second on a wild pitch to win the second game after wrapping up the opener with a sacfly.

These were exciting fans, noisy and very young, and in the first game they grew a bit obstreperous. There was a duster duel between Tom Seaver and Bill Hands. They pinged each other with pitches in the third.

Ump Frank Secory shook a warning finger at Seaver, and here came Gil Hodges, who is supposed not to get hypertense about such things.

The throbbing noises, the chants of "we-want-a-hit," the decibilic pressures, did not seem to get to the Met pitchers. Both Tom Seaver and Tug McGraw went all the way. McGraw was a sub starter for sore-fingered Jim McAndrew, and the Tugger did a tremendous gutty job, surviving nine hits, including two in the ninth that put the knotter on third.

It seemed, at the start, McGraw wouldn't survive the first. The Mets had rapped Dick Selma for two in their first, and the Cubs banged back to get two in the bottom half on three straight hits.

Selma, a Met in Cub clothing, wild-pitched home the winning run in the seventh.

That makes Lefty McGraw 3-and-0. Righty Seaver is 3-and-2 with his first game job. He, too, gutted a nine-hitter.

N. Y. Mets second baseman Ken Boswell shows an arm which was nicked by a pitch in the eighth inning. The wild pitch put Ken on first to load the bases, then Cleon Jones belted his first major league grand-slam.

Al Spangler's ribby triple got him for a run in the second. Then Ed Kranepool shot his No. 3 into the right bleachers to knot things in the fourth, and the next stanza Seaver walked to open the winning rally. Hits by Rod Gaspar and Ken Boswell scored him, then a sacrifice line-out by Swoboda made it 3-1. ∎

Four Home Runs Help Mets Turn Back Reds

by Red Foley

Don Cardwell pitched and batted the Mets to an 8-1 runaway win over the Reds before 12,291 chilled onlookers at Shea Stadium last night. The victory, gained at the expense of reliever Gary Nolan, was Cardy's first after four defeats.

The big right-hander, who started against no-hit Jim Maloney, yielded six hits and slugged a three-run homer to cap the five-run eighth that blew the thing wide open.

Neither Maloney nor Cardwell was perfect, but both were good enough for the first three frames. Gaspar marred Maloney's plans of emulating double no-hit Johnny Vandemeer when he cracked the second serve for two bases into the right corner.

Gaspar reached third with two outs but was stranded when Jones rolled to Perez. Harrelson's leadoff single in the third was Maloney's only other defection. But the shortstop never moved off first as the Reds' righty disposed of the next three. Johnson's two-out single in the first was Cincy's only hit as Cardwell unveiled a strikeout pitch that saw him register five K's in the first four rounds.

Boswell, one of the six lefty swingers in Hodges' lineup, nudged Cardwell into a 1-0 edge when he led the fourth with a soaring shot into the Mets' pen in right. Jones followed with a walk and stole second with two out. But he stayed there as Swoboda tapped to Woodward at short.

With one out in the fifth, May squared it when he rammed Cardwell's 3-2 serve on a buzzing line over the wall in left-center. After getting Helms on a loft to center, Cardwell yielded a single to Woodward before dispensing of Maloney on a tap to Boswell.

Harrelson's boot on Rose's leadoff grounder put Cardy into a mild jam in the sixth. After Tolan forced Rose, the former swiped second, but advanced no further. After Bench walked, Cardwell got Perez on a fly to Swoboda.

Nolan relieved Maloney in the sixth. It was suspected the latter reinjured the groin muscle he pulled while running the bases in the eighth inning of his no-hitter last Wednesday against Houston. Garrett and Jones, sandwiching Boswell's grounder, made it 3-1 with solo shots over the right wall. Garrett's was the rookie's maiden major league homer; Jones' was his No. 4.

May led the Reds' seventh with a two-bagger into the left corner, but went no further because Cardwell retired Helms, Woodward and Stewart, swinging for Nolan. Granger was serving when Harrelson doubled and Cardwell singled on a topped ball down the third-base line. Gaspar's tap to May advanced them before Granger got Garrett on a foul for the third out. ∎

Tug: Way to a Man's Success in Baseball Is Home Cooking

by Norm Miller

Tug McGraw, ex-scatterarm, ex-flake and ex-bachelor playboy, yesterday detailed the secret of his 3-0 success. It is, Tug explained, the serenity of married life in a basement apartment in Flushing with a bride who has charm, looks, understands baseball and can cook, too.

It is all part of growing up, Tug philosophized on the Mets' day off. A guy has to mature as a man to mature as a pitcher. And that is the story behind the 24-year-old lefty who has worked his way into the Mets' starting rotation with three straight wins and 24 strikeouts in less than 23 innings.

Success, says Tug McGraw, is born of many-splendored things. It is married life; the man-to-man counsel of Bill Virdon and Larry Bearnarth during two seasons in the minors; it is a screwball pitch taught by Ralph Terry, and the outgrowing of a screwball attitude.

"Mostly it's being married," McGraw said. "I have a lot more time to think about baseball than when I was single. I used to go out a lot and fool around quite a bit. Now I come home to Mama," he smiled. "We have more serious things to talk about."

"Mama" is wife Phyllis, a one-time TWA stewardess whom Tug met in Mister Laffs, Phil Linz' meeting grounds for the young smart set. They were married last June 1.

McGraw insists he is firing the ball right now harder than when he first came up to the Mets as a wild 19-year-old. The reason, he says, is added weight. And the weight, he insists, was put on by wifie's home cooking.

"When I first joined the Mets, I weighed 165," McGraw said. "Last year, before I was married, I weighed 170. Now I'm 190. It's not fat at all but good, solid weight. Phyllis is a tremendous cook. She's the best cook a man could want."

McGraw owes his spot in the starting rotation to two tremendous long relief jobs and the arm miseries of Jerry Koosman. He realizes the Mets' need for a lefty reliever could send him right back to the bullpen when Koosman returns. The thought does not disturb him.

"I was extremely happy in the bullpen," he said. "The biggest thrill I've had—outside the game in which I beat Sandy Koufax—was that relief job against the Cubs (April 27)."

He referred to the game in which he relieved Jim McAndrew, worked his way out of a no-out jam, and went on to get the win after four hitless innings." ■

may '69

Mets: From Ridiculous to Sublime

8 Runs in 8th Slam Braves, 9-3

by Joe O'Day

 **T**ruth is stranger than fiction, but the Mets are beyond explanation. No-hit for six innings and absolutely helpless, the Mets rallied for eight runs in the eighth inning to trounce the Braves, 9-3, last night at Shea Stadium before a disbelieving crowd of 15,365.

Right-hander Phil Niekro, the winningest picture in the NL with a 6-1 record, really flirted with fame. The 30-year-old had a lot going for him, like a perfect game for one out into the fifth; a no-hitter going into the seventh and finally his seventh victory going into the fateful eighth when it went Pffft.

The knuckleballing Niekro was staked to a three-run lead after dueling Tom Seaver through five scoreless innings. It looked like a slaughter as Seaver was touched for a pair of runs in the sixth and another in the seventh on Felipe Alou's third homer of the season.

The fans and the Mets awoke suddenly in the seventh as Ken Boswell with a triple to center field, and Cleon Jones spoiled the shutout a moment later with a ground out.

The start of the rally was typically Mets, as Amos Otis fanned but reached first when rookie catcher Bob Didier was charged with a passed ball. Bud Harrelson then pulled a single through the right side, and it was a first and third situation with the recalled Art Shamsky swinging for Seaver.

Shamsky hit a comebacker to Niekro, who bluffed Otis back to third, and then threw to second.

Shortstop Sonny Jackson dropped the ball and the bases were loaded. Tommie Agee jumped on a fast ball for a double to left, chasing in Otis and Harrelson with the tying runs, and Niekro left talking to himself.

Southpaw George Stone came on to purposely pass Ed Charles, pinch-hitting for Garrett, and the bases were loaded again. Then Stone nicked Boswell on the forearm to force in Al Weis, running for Shamsky.

Plate umpire Billy Williams at first called it a strike, but manager Gil Hodges led the charge to the plate. Hodges, Boswell and coaches Yogi Berra and Eddie Yost convinced the arbiter. Then Stone really got rocked.

Jones got into the first pitch and rammed his sixth homer of the season over the left-field fence. It was also his first grand slam. Still, the Mets were not content, as J.C. Martin tripled and tallied on a wild pitch by Stone, who by this time was just so much clay.

The eight-run outburst equaled the club record for an inning, set against this same team, June 26, 1964, when the Braves franchise was in Milwaukee. ∎

Jones Brushes off Jammed Ankle; Grote Sits

by Dick Young

Cleon Jones limped on and off the charter that flew the Mets here today and when Cleon limps, the Mets worry. "Don't worry," said Cleon. "I'll tape it up and play tonight." He meant the ankle.

Jerry Grote, another of the walking wounded, wasn't so sure. He had been banged on the right hand by a pitch yesterday, and it was puffed just behind the knuckles. "I'll take some heat and get some sound soon as I get out to the park," he said. "When it happened, I thought the knuckles were smashed." X-rays taken this morning show no break.

Gil Hodges was willing to settle for Jones and give Grote a rest. The manager said J.C. Martin would catch Tug McGraw tonight. It's easier to sit down a Grote batting .181 than a Jones batting .390.

Cleon jammed his left ankle on a steal of second yesterday. He has what they call a chronic ankle. Every so often it flares up under inordinate strain.

"You tape it up for a week," says trainer Gus Mauch, "and then you take off the tape. Either way, he keeps right on going, and as fast as he can run with it is amazing." Mauch expects Jones will have some ankle trouble, on and off, the rest of his playing days. ■

DAILY NEWS Frank Hurley

Mets outfielder Cleon Jones makes a try for a shoestring catch.

may '69

Kooz Coos Pennant Lullaby

by Dick Young

*J*erry Koosman is so high, psychologically, he is predicting a pennant for the Mets. "I think this proves we have a pennant contender, he said today, following last night's test of his precious left arm, and of Jim McAndrews' right.*

"Now all we need," said Kooz, "is for Nolan to come back, and we'll give those Cubs a battle," Nolan is Nolan Ryan, third part of the decimated Met staff, which has held up so admirably through it all. Ryan is on the disabled list with a pulled groin; due off it when the three-week minimum expires 10 days hence.

Kooz was the big one, and he passed it with flying K's. The test was at Memphis, where the Mets last night played their Texas League farm club. Kooz worked five innings as scheduled, and fanned 10. The nagging question is: was it Kooz's fastball or the Memphis lights?

"He looked very good," said Rube Walker, the pitching coach. "I don't care about these strikeouts or the lights. All I know is there was no sign of anything wrong with his shoulder. He came straight overhand, and about 75% of his fastballs were very good. When he tried to overthrow, he didn't get good stuff on the ball."

Jim Andrews' trouble has been a blistered fingertip, the so-called curve ball blister. It went deep and left a slow-healing hole. He was out of action two days before Koosman.

This leaves Nolan Ryan and his pulled groin muscle. The Mets think they have the best pitching, the deepest pitching in the league. The hitting has perked up, and with Kooz and McAndrews back, they speak of making a run at the Cubs.

"I don't think Chicago or anybody can play that good all year long," says Koosman, referring to the .649 pace that has put the Cubs six lengths up on the Mets.

"Somebody is going to start catching up with them, and I think we will the next time we play them." ■

Jerry Koosman (left) with Mets owner Mrs. Joan Payson.

Mets Go with Seaver for Stab at .500

by Dick Young

With their first legitimate .500 record as the goal, the Amazin' Mets today made a pertinent pitching switch. They named Tom Seaver to start tonight, instead of lefty Tug McGraw, the original nominee. Seaver started the last game played by the Mets, two days ago, and was saved by the rain while trailing, 3-0, in the middle of the fourth.

"We figured," said Rube Walker, pitching coach, after talking it over with Gil Hodges, "that Seaver had thrown only four innings. Hell, that's like throwing batting practice, and then coming back two days later and pitching. That's all he's doing this way."

Counting pitches is a big item with the Mets. Everything is judged on number of pitches. They, rather than innings, indicate the strain on a pitching arm, particularly a young pitching arm, which is what the Mets have most of.

The other cardinal rule applied by Rube Walker and Gil Hodges is this: Pitch Tom Seaver whenever he's ready, and fit in everyone else accordingly.

There's a special incentive this time. By winning this game, the Mets would be 18-and-18. Never, past 4-and-4, have they been at .500 in the seven-plus years of their struggling existence.

Almost as obvious as the fact that the Mets are a better club is the realization that their luck has changed. And perhaps the two go together. As they come into Atlanta, the Braves are in bad physical shape. Felipe Alou has been hit on the hand with a pitch, Orlando Cedpeda is recovering from a beanball, and Tito Francona has a dislocated thumb. ∎

m a y ' 6 9

National League Eastern Division

As of May 21

Team	Wins	Losses	Percentage	Games Back
Chicago	25	13	.658	—
Pittsburgh	18	18	.500	6
METS	17	18	.486	6 1/2
St. Louis	17	19	.471	7
Philadelphia	15	19	.411	8
Montreal	11	22	.333	11 1/2

Mets at .500 as Seaver 3-Hits Braves, 5-0

by Dick Young

With the help of somebody up there and a couple of guys down here, the Amazin' Mets tonight reached the unreachable plateau. They are, for the first time in their seven-plus years of travel and travail, at .500, after beating the Braves and knuckler Phil Niekro, 5-0.

The guys down here who did it were Tom Seaver, with a three-hitter that makes him five straight and 6-2; Cleon Jones, who drove in two runs in the first, added another hit and now is batting .391 with 30 ribbys and Bud Harrelson, who tripled with the bags full to take the pressure off Seaver in the eighth. Till these three, Bud had only six ribbys.

When you speak about being .500 for the first time, you mean once the race gets straightened away; not counting the unsettled first week or so. Earlier Mets had been 2 and 2, 3 and 3, once even 4 and 4, but class told. Now, in their new image, they are 18 and 18, and climbing.

DAILY NEWS Dan Farrell

Tom Seaver delivers. His 3-hit win put the Mets at the .500 mark for the first time.

National League Eastern Division
As of May 22

Team	Wins	Losses	Percentage	Games Back
Chicago	25	14	.641	—
Pittsburgh	19	18	.514	6
METS	18	18	.500	7
St. Louis	17	20	.459	7
Philadelphia	15	20	.429	8
Montreal	11	23	.324	11 1/2

may '69

Mets Put off Bubbly: It's First Place or Bust!

by Dick Young

here was no champagne in the Mets' clubhouse last night. Some of the guys settled for the self-service Bud on draft that has been installed in the visitors' clubhouse here, and that was it. It was all very ordinary, very low key, almost a put-on. You'd think the Mets played .500 all the time.*

"What's to get excited about?" said Tom Merriwell, who sometimes goes by the name of Tom Seaver. "We haven't done anything yet. You go get Marv Throneberry and Richie Ashburn and the rest of those original Mets and have a champagne party with them, then come back in September when we clinch first place and celebrate with us."

Tom Seaver was talking to newsmen, those ever-loving romanticists who seemed more impressed than the ballplayers with the fact that the Mets had, at last, reached the unreachable plateau.

"You may take it lightly," protested a regular Met correspondent, "but you haven't suffered through the entire seven years the way some of us have. You're a Johnny-come-lately." Seaver is in his fourth season.

"Ask some of the guys who have lived it," said another newsman. "Ask Al Jackson there."

"What do you mean?" said Ed Kranepool. "He picked up a World Series check in St. Louis two years ago." It was a reference to the fact that Jackson, although an original Met, had been traded to the Cardinals for two seasons before returning to Shea.

"That's right," said Jackson, beaming. "Life is lovelier the second time around." ■

Like Old Times: Mets Fall, 15-3

May 23, 1969
by Dick Young

The rarified air on the .500 plateau was just too thin for the Mets to inhale for any length of time. Less than 24 hours after they had achieved the highest pinnacle in their eight-year history, the Amazins were pushed back down again by the cocky Braves, who made a little history themselves in their 15-3 romp by lifting Henry Aaron for a pinch-hitter for the first time in his 16-year career.

The distinction of being the first man ever to bat for Aaron went to Mike Lum, a Chinese-Hawaiian outfielder, which was really rubbing it in. Lum, a lefthanded hitter, was sent up against the lefthanded Jackson but Mike showed his respect for the honor of the occasion by belting Alvin's first pitch for a two-run double.

Kooz' Return a Met Must

by Dick Young

Tonight's Met game against the hot Astros is quite important to Gil Hodges. Not alone because it can stem the Mets' two-notch backslide from the .500 high mark, but also because much could depend upon the pitching comeback of Jerry Koosman, who is making his first start in almost a month.

It has become increasingly apparent that the Mets cannot make a serious move without Koosman back in the rotation. They cannot do it with Tom Seaver alone. They need the one-two pitch punch they had last season in order to show continued improvement.

Gary Gentry and Tug McGraw are not ready to pick up the slack. Their earlier contributions to the situation were laudable, but of late Genry has shown an alarming tendency to make careless, costly pitches, and McGraw has returned to the reality that he does not have staying power. Other than an occasional spot start, McGraw must resign himself to being a reliever.

Koosman's comeback blueprint calls for him to make 100 pitches or so tonight, then pack it in. This has been decided in meetings among Kooz, pitching coach Rube Walker and manager Hodges. It is a safeguard against a recurrence of the shoulder condition that sidelined Koosman April 29.

"I doubt very much they'll let me go nine," Koosman said this afternoon. He laughed. "I hope I'm not pitching a no-hitter with one out in the ninth when they jerk me because I've thrown 100 pitches," he said. ∎

Pitcher Jerry Koosman works on his bunting at batting practice.

may '69

Padres Give No Consolation as Mets Lose 4th in a Row

by Joe Trimble

A crowd of about 12,000 came out in the wind at Shea Stadium last night for what looked like a road showing of Les Miserables. The Mets opened an eight-game home stand with their first game against the expansion Padres.

If it is true that misery loves company, then this was a meeting of two unhappy companions. San Diego had lost 29 games, most in either league, including 11 of its last 13. The Mets, after reaching the .500 level at 18-18, dropped four straight on their recent trip.

The pitching match paired losers, righthander Al Santorini (1-2) for the visitors against Jim McAndrew (0-1). Santorini, from Union, New Jersey, had not started in 11 days due to a tight shoulder. McAndrew had been bothered for exactly a month with a blistered middle finger and this was his first start since April 27.

The Mets had managed to keep an even keel on the road, 10 and 10, but had a home deficit of 8-12 to be four games under .500.

McAndrew got himself in a bit of a jam in the first inning when Sippin singled and Gonzales walked with one out, but he got Colbert to bounce into a double play.

The Mets moved right off to a scant lead through a surprise play. Agee singled to right and was on second with two out when Jones singled to short.

Mets, SD Open Shea 2-Set

May 28, 1969
by Joe Trimble

If it is true that misery loves company, then the Mets and the Padres made a miserably companionable pair last night at Shea Stadium. The old expansionists and the new ones opened a two-game series, their first contact with one another.

Agee got to third. Kranepool then surprised with a perfect bunt down the third-base line, unplayable, as Agee scored. Swoboda ended it by bouncing back to the pitcher.

The Padres got bank in a hurry, Ollie Brown driving his seventh homer over the 371-foot mark in left-center as the second inning began. Clarence Gaston added a double before McAndrew got out of the inning. ■

Kooz Fans 15 but Tug Gets Mets' Credit, 1-0

by Joe Trimble

Jerry Koosman set Met history with 15 strikeouts last night at Shea Stadium as the Mets broke their five-game losing sreak with a 1-0 win over the Padres in 11 innings . . . and didn't get the victory. That went to Tug McGraw in relief.

The tall southpaw starter fanned 14 in eight innings to tie Nolan Ryan's club record, didn't get a whiff in the ninth and then picked up No. 15, most by one Metsie in one contest in the club's lifetime, in the tenth.

Kooz retired for a pinch hitter in the home half of the tenth and McGraw got through the eleventh, although he walked two. That left-hander was saved by an alert play by catcher Jerry Grote, who snatched up a bunt and fired to second to start a double play.

Koosman's toughest inning was the second. Ollie Brown walked and Nate Colbert singled him to second. Roberto Pena's bunt moved up the runners. Kooz then whiffed Clarence Gaston, walked catcher Chris Cannizzaro on purpose and struck out Kirby on three pitches.

Ryan got his 14 K's in nine innings against Cincy here on May 14 last year. Koosman's 15 are an NL high by one pitcher this season, surpassing Larry Dierker's 14 for Houston against the Phils on May 17. ∎

Gil Sets All-Righty Lineup for Giants' McCormick

May 30, 1969
by Joe Trimble

With the loss of regular second baseman and No. 3 slot hitter Ken Boswell to the Army for two weeks, Gil Hodges is giving the Mets' lineup its most radical shakeup of the season tonight when the Giants move into Shea Stadium.

"I think it can be a winning lineup," the manager said with a grin yesterday as the team went through a workout in 95 degrees.

He will have the shortstop Bud Harrelson lead off, followed by Rod Gaspar in right field, Tommy Agee in center, Cleon Jones on first, Ron Swoboda in left, Ed Charles at third, Jerry Grote catching and Al Weis on second.

This gives him an all-righty batting order against San Francisco southpaw Mike McCormick, who holds a 6-2 lieftime edge over the Mets.

With Tom Seaver pitching, McCormick will have to contend with nine righthanded batters. In addition, there will be two righty reserves available in Duffy Dyer and Amos Otis. Four lefty swingers will be available in the event they are needed: Wayne Garrett, J.C. Martin, Ed Kranepool and Art Shamsky.

The new batting order represents Gil's most extraordinary use of the platoon system so far this year.

In addition to Boswell's absence, it removes two other regulars from the batting order. Garrett at third, and Kranepool at first.

DAILY NEWS

Jerry Grote

Grote's Temper Met Sore Spot

by Dick Young

Jerry Grote wasn't always a hot-headed catcher. He used to be a hot-headed pitcher.

You watch the arm, and you can see it. It's a good arm. It was exceptional when he first came up. Everybody in the league talked about it. The gun, they'd say. What a gun!

Jerry Grote will tell you the gun isn't quite what it was when he came up to Houston five years ago. Or even the arm the Mets got in the winter of '65, when they gave Tom Parsons (Tom Parsons?) and some money for it.

"It's about this much shorter," he says, and he holds his hands about a foot apart. This is the way ballplayers describe velocity of a throw by a pitcher or a catcher; by the distance it travels with same amount of effort and in the same elapsed time. They talk of a pitcher losing this-much off his fast ball. Grote's arm can be this-much-shorter, and still be one of the best in the league.

Grote has lost something off his temper, too. He used to fight the umpires, his pitchers, and himself.

One of the first things Gil Hodges did upon becoming Mets manager was talk to Jerry Grote about it. He called him into the clubhouse office at St. Petersburg after an intra-squad game. You have to be something else to get on an umpire in an intra-squad game.

"You're not doing what you're capable of doing to help the pitcher," Hodges remembers telling him.

"I know, but that friggin umpire . . .," Grote started.

"They have a tough job to do, anyway, without climbing all over them," said Hodges. "There is a time to argue. If you think he has blown one, tell him. Then get it over with. You have to be more concerned with the course of a game. You have to think about situations. There's more to catching than putting down one finger, and here comes the fast ball. You can't get all riled up."

Grote said he would try to change. He did. He also changed his style of hitting. He cut down on his swing, went to the opposite field with the pitch away from him. He changed so much he made the All-Star team, first string. This year, Jerry Grote did not make the All-Star team. He back-slid. The temper shows again; not so much with the umpires as with his teammates. He gets sore at the pitcher for a mistake. He fires the ball back, sometimes harder than the pitcher threw it to him. Hodges had to tell Grote about that, too.

For a good catcher, an agile catcher, Grote will make unbelievable mistakes. The other night in Houston, the runner broke from third. It was a squeeze. Ron Taylor, the pitcher, reacted. He fired the ball high and tight, the knockdown pitch. There's a saying in baseball: you can't bunt when you're on your back. The ducking batter couldn't touch the ball. Neither did Grote. Lunging forward, as if to meet the runner, Grote failed to come out of his crouch. The pitch flew overhead, past the stretching mitt, and the runner scored easily with a big run. The Mets blew another to the Astros.

Tips on Catching

When a pitch is in the dirt, slap it in front of you. Keep yourself lined up in back of the ball. It'll hit off your chest and lay there, and the man on base won't run. There's something psychological about the runner seeing the ball where you also can see it. It can be 20 feet in front of you and he won't run, but if it's four feet in back of you, he'll take off. One other thing: wear a cup.

—Jerry Grote

Cleon Jones leaps against the bullpen screen in Shea Stadium's left field in an attempt to catch the ball hit by Willie Mays.

The Mets were beginning to prove that their .500 record was no fluke. And all of New York City was asking itself, "Who are these guys? And what have they done with our Amazin' Mets?"

Not only did Jerry Koosman throw a five-hitter against the Dodgers to get the Mets back to .500, but Ed Kranepool drove two out of the park to help put the Mets in second place in the division. The Mets actually tallied their first winning record past the first week of the season.

The Mets weren't done yet. They put together an 11-game winning streak that was finally stopped by the Giants. It was the longest streak in the majors that year, not to mention the franchise's longest streak.

As surprise began to be replaced with respect by the rest of baseball, the Mets made a move to get the offensive reinforcements they were looking for. They needed a slugger, and a slugger they got.

Midway through June, the Mets traded four young players to the Montreal Expos for the veteran slugger Donn Clendenon. Clendenon had retired before the season, then become the center of a dispute between the Expos and Astros, before unretiring and signing with Montreal. The Mets' trade for offense paid dividends quickly. Clendenon drove in the lead run or the winning run in his first 16 games.

And as if Koosman and Seaver weren't enough trouble for opposing batters, Nolan Ryan was back from the disabled list and hurling heat.

Mets Walk over Giants, 5-4; Sweep Series

by Norm Miller

*R*on Swoboda won it in a walk yesterday, a simple, patient stroll right into that thin book of historic Met accomplishments. Ron's bases-loaded, two-out walk off Joe Gibbon in the ninth inning forced in the run that gave the Mets a 5-4 win and their first three-game series sweep ever against the Giants.

Four walks in that ninth inning carved this chunk of history before a delirious crowd of 41,294. Four walks sent Bud Harrelson jogging home with the run that swept the series with the Giants, and every game was a come-from-behind win. This latest four-win streak has the Mets one game below .500 again.

It was a three-hour plus duel in which the Mets twice before had come from behind with two-run bursts off Bob Bolin, in which their starter, Jim McAndrew, left the game in the second with a blistered middle pitching finger, in which the Giants' Willie McCovey hit his 16th homer, and which wound up as win No. 1 for Ron Taylor, who had saved the opening game of this set Friday night.

The Mets have swept an occasional three-game series, the latest against the Dodgers last June, but never before from the Giants.

Twice the Mets had come from behind this sunny afternoon, the first time tying the score at 2-2 in the second on Jerry Grote's two-run triple and later moving ahead, 4-3, in the fifth on RBI singles by Ed Kranepool and Swoboda. ■

DAILY NEWS George Mattson

Ron Swoboda didn't need to take a swing to beat the Giants. He did it with a walk.

june '69

Kooz 5-Hits LA, 2-1; Mets at .500

by Red Foley

Jerry Koosman may have been singing "I Got Plenty of Nuthin'," but the Dodgers were moaning the blues when the super southpaw, pitching out of a ninth-inning jam, hurled the Mets back to .500 with a superb 2-1 triumph before 23,600 appreciative Shea onlookers last night.

"I didn't have my good curve and my fastball, while it was good, wasn't going where I wanted it to," the 25-year-old Koosman said in the victorious clubhouse. "I didn't have my rhythm, but I will say when they got that man to third I was able to reach back and fire."

Koosman had gotten the two runs he needed back in the fourth and they were the kind the old Mets used to give up rather than get. With two out and Cleon Jones on, via a force, Dodger lefty Claude Osteen walked Charles on four straight pitches. He then got Jerry Grote to lift what should have been an inning-ending pop to third.

But the gusty gales played havoc with the ball and Sudakis reeled around the left side of the infield before the wind-whipped ball fell behind his jacknife-dive. ■

june '69

Never, but Never, Have Mets Been So Good So Late

by Larry Fox

om Seaver took the Shea Stadium mound last night with a chance to grasp history in his strong right paw. The Mets, in all their born days (this is their eighth year) never have been above the .500 mark in the standings. If he beats the Dodgers, they would be 24-23 with a six-game winning streak.

The word "never" requires a minor note of explanation, sort of a small asterisk. They were 2-1 in the first week of the 1966 season.

Usually, they started most years in a perennial slump, diving into the cellar to stay. Only twice did they yield the cellar, to the Cubs in 1966 and to the Astros last season.

The six-game string, if attained, would be the second best in their history. In July of 1966, they got giddy and reeled off seven in succession.

Seaver (7-3) faced righhander Alan Foster, young speedballer who was looking for his first victory after two losses.

It was Tom who got them up to .500 on May 21, when he beat Atlanta for 18-18. Then, true to their fashion, the Metsies went into a spin and dropped five in succession. But they rebounded and Jerry Koosman's brilliant 2-1 win over the Dodgers Monday night brought them back to an even keel again. ∎

National League Eastern Division

As of June 5

Team	Wins	Losses	Percentage	Games Back
Chicago	35	16	.686	—
METS	24	23	.511	9
Pittsburgh	25	24	.510	9
St. Louis	24	26	.480	10 1/2
Philadelphia	18	27	.400	14
Montreal	11	34	.244	21

Mets Sitting on Cloud Two, but for How Long?

by Joe Trimble

ave the Mets crossed the Great Divide? Have they discarded the harlequin image of the clown and donned the cloth of respectability? In other words, have they become a major league team? Are they for real?

Nobody knows. Gil Hodges said softly after the sixth-straight victory Tuesday night: "They are playing ball the way I thought they might be able to."

Asked if it was time to break out the champagne, the manager semi-smiled and answered. "Maybe there will be a time soon to consider it."

The Mets are over the .500 level for the first time in their time. They made their happy history Tuesday night with a 5-2 win over the Dodgers to be 24-23...the only time, considering it realistically, they ever have been better than worse. In the first week of 1966, they managed a 2-1 before reverting to form.

Tuesday's win over the Dodgers moved the Mets into second place ahead of the Pirates. Second place. Have they gone nuts?

Even with the surge to success, they remain their independently erratic selves. Ed Charles and Ron Swoboda carried the club in the early part of the current streak, while Cleon Jones slumped and Ed Kranepool and rookie Wayne Garrett played so-so or didn't play at all. ■

Ryan Back— but no Starts Yet

June 8, 1969
by Joe Trimble

The rich get richer or the good get better . . . or something. Anyway, the Mets, riding the crest of a wave of success higher and happier than ever in their history, added another strong arm today.

The better way to say it is that they regained the arm—the flame-throwing right one which belongs to Nolan Ryan, who was placed on the active list.

Nolan, 22, worked out impressively prior to last night's record-shattering eighth straight victory, a 5-3 come-from-behind effort against the Padres. He threw so hard that he had the hitters "ouching" from the stings in their hands when he hit their bats. They told him to cool off.

Ryan had been on the disabled list (a minimum of 21 days) since sustaining a groin injury while pitching one-third of an inning against the Astros at home on May 11. He threw only one pitch, causing Jesus Alou to pop out and end the fifth inning.

"I believe it was the hardest pitch I ever saw him throw," manager Gil Hodges recalled today. "And when he threw it we (Hodges and pitching coach Rube Walker) knew he had hurt himself. We got him right into the clubhouse after he came to the bench and the doctor's examination showed that he was really hurt."

So lush are the Mets in the pitching art that there is no place in the starting setup for him right now. Jerry Koosman went after the ninth in a row tonight and Tom Seaver is Sunday's child. The aces back-to-back may bring the wild winning ways to 10 in a row. Best ever, previously, was seven (July 17-22, 1966).

Mets No. 10

3-2 over San Diego

by Joe Trimble

It used to be said that a human would land on the moon before the Mets became a decent ball club. Oh, yeah? Well, maybe the Magnificent Metsies will beat the astronauts to lunar land. Here, today, they kept flying high as they beat the Padres.

The pitching has been unbelievable during this ascension into orbit. Tom Seaver struck out 14 in seven innings today, and Ron Taylor in two hitless relief rounds to lock up Seaver's ninth victory.

Here, last night, as the Mets won, 4-1, Jerry Koosman whiffed 11. Friday night, Gary Gentry struck out eight.

Over the 10-game span, the staff has fanned 98 in 89 innings and has allowed but 58 hits and 16 earned runs.

The longest winning streak in club history began almost two weeks ago with a win over San Diego at Shea Stadium, May 28. Since then, the Flushing Fantastiks have swept a three-game series with three California teams—the Giants, Dodgers and Padres, in that order.

The best the Mets ever did in a 10-game interval in the past was eight out of 10. And their previous high win-string was seven, July 17-22, 1966.

In this zoom-boom, they have scored as many as five runs only three times and have allowed four runs in a game but once. ■

Walt: Mets Have Matured

June 10, 1969
by Joe Trimble

Break up the Mets! They are getting to be too much, with their 10-game winning streak, overpowering pitching, almost flawless fielding and come-from-behind, late-inning rallies. They are five games over .500 and no longer are funny. At long last, they have become a quality ball club. They are the best expansion team in major league history, beyond a doubt.

Through a distillation process, of which 178 players have come and gone, a residue of solid people has resulted. It took eight years and much patience, by the fans as well as the front office, to bring them to the point where, as Dodger manager Walter Alston says: "They've grown up. They no longer beat themselves. They hold on to one-run leads and they make the big plays."

That's his way of saying that this team has matured. And it is still young and most of the players will be around for many years.

With the exception of Agee, a pickup from the White Sox, and Grote, obtained from Houston, all are home grown—a tribute to the farm system directors of the Mets, Joe McDonald and Whitey Herzog.

Mets' 11th Majors' Best, 9-4

Agee (2), Cleon homer

by Joe Trimble

*T**he majestic Mets now own the longest winning streak in the majors this year. No kidding, they do. They jolted the Giants, 9-4, for their eleventh straight victory tonight as Tommie Agee belted two homers and Cleon Jones one.***

Agee had four of the 13 hits in the easiest win of the streak. The nine runs was the most the Shea stunners have scored in the great grab and the margin of five runs was also the largest. Six of the wins have come by one run, two by two and two by three.

The victims have all been California teams, four each against San Diego and San Francisco and three over Los Angeles.

This, of course, is the longest winning string in club history, by four. It also beat the 1969 winning run of 10 by Houston.

Don Cardwell got his second victory but couldn't finish it after holding a two-hitter over eight frames. Homers by Willie McCovey and Jack Hiatt kayoed him and Ron Taylor finished it up.

The Mets simply have matured, to become the best expansion club ever. In their history, 178 players have worn the uniform. The distillation finally has produced a quality product.

The Giants got two walks to the Willies, Mays and McCovey, in the first but Davenport flied out. They got nothing in the third on McCormick's single through the box and Bonds' triple to right center.

Agee evened it with one stroke in the fourth, crashing a homer over the centerfield fence, some 420 feet distant. It was his eighth.

They took the lead in the following inning on two long drives. Grote doubled to deep left-center, moved to third on Weis' bunt and came in when Cardwell backed leftfielder Ken Henderson to the fence for his near-homer. ■

Can't Win 'Em All: Mets Flop, 7-2

by Joe Trimble

The Mets reverted to form today, becoming the happy hooligans we all have come to know and love. They laid their 11-game winning streak on the line and the Giants stomped it, 7-2.

Five Met pitchers were bombed for a dozen hits, Willie Mays and Ron Hunt getting three a piece. Willie McCovey only had two but he also drew three of the nine walks handed out as his average jumped to .355. That figure tied him for the league lead with Pittsburgh's Matty Alou.

Gaylord Perry held off both the Mets and plate ump Doug Harvey. He allowed only four hits, one a homer by Ed Kranepool after the score was 7-0 in the seventh.

Harvey spent much of the day looking for the grease the Jint righthander was supposed to use on the ball. Under a new edict by NL prexy Warren Giles, the pitcher can be ejected if he is doctoring up the ball, in the ump's judgment. Harvey threw three balls out of the game but not the pitcher.

In New York on May 31, manager Gil Hodges noticed some sort of clear jelly on the balls thrown

DAILY NEWS Frank Hurley

Gaylord Perry and the Giants ended the Mets club record winning streak at 11. Here, Perry covers home plate.

by Perry and gave the plate ump Frank Secory a five-minute lecture about it but was told that nothing could be done about it as the league office would not back them up. ■

Mets Obtain Clendenon for Four Farmhands

by Joe Trimble

The Mets swung a major deal today and used minor league players to swing it. They obtained slugger Donn Clendenon from Montreal for four youngsters in their farm system.

Clendenon, 33, will report to the Metsies for Tuesday night's twi-niter in Philly. Gil Hodges said he will platoon the right-handed batter at first base with Ed Kranepool.

"We'll see how it goes from there," the manager added, indicating that if the veteran hits, he will also play him in the outfield against right-handers.

Of the four given up, only infielder Kevin Collins has major league experience. The other three are right-handed pitchers: Steve Renko, 24, Jay Carden, 25, and Dave Colon, 19. Collins is 22 and a good prospect. GM Johnny Murphy doesn't think much of the others.

Murphy insisted on talking with Clendenon before finalizing the deal because Donn threatened to quit baseball after being traded by Houston to Montreal and go into business as an executive with a pen company in Atlanta, where he lives.

"He said that all that is past now," Murphy said. "He insists that he is dedicated to baseball and even offered to sign a five-year contract. I'd like one of those, too." ■

DAILY NEWS   John Duprey

Donn Clendenon made his presence felt immediately. He drove in the leading or winning run in his first 16 games.

june '69

Donn Glad to Don Met Suit

by Joe Trimble

Donn Clendenon is happy to be a Met and very enthused at being with Gil Hodges, who he calls "my idol." The big slugger was obtained in a swap with the Expos Sunday afternoon and will be at first base in tomorrow night's opener of a twin bill with the Phillies against lefthander Grant Jackson.

"I was having trouble in the field a few years ago," Donn recalled yesterday. "Gil was managing the Senators. So, before an exhibition game, I got the guts to go over and ask him to help me. I think that no right-handed first baseman could find a better fielder to copy himself after.

"Gil is the kind of a man who won't walk over and offer advice. But if you ask it, he will give you all the help he can. I had 'stiff hands.' I had been told to use both hands in taking the throws.

"Gil said that wasn't necessary. He showed me how to relax my hand and catch the ball with the glove. And I hope that I'm not enough of a nut at 33 to think he can't help me some more. I'm sure he can teach me more than I know now and I want to keep learning from him."

Clendenon admits he wasn't comfortable in Montreal. "I don't think I ever really fitted into their plans," he said. "They took me in the expansion (from Pittsburgh) and then traded me (to Houston) before I ever played for them. Then when they are in a long, losing streak, they didn't play me much. I don't see how a .280 lifetime hitter who has knocked in a lot of runs should be sitting on the bench of an expansion team which was losing. ∎

> "I don't see how a .280 lifetime hitter who has knocked in a lot of runs should be sitting on the bench of an expansion team which was losing."
>
> —Donn Clendenon

Would You Believe 3 1/2 back of Mets?

by Norm Miller

n opening day, 63 games ago, what hallucination could have envisioned the champ Cardinals coming to town trailing the Mets by 3 1/2 games? Red Schoendienst, who qualifies as an expert on NL standings, had a few thoughts last night on this wild fantasy.

Actually, it is only half-fantasy, Red analyzed. The Mets, 5 1/2 games out of first as they opened a four-game set at Shea, are for real. It is his Cardinals, nine games out, who are out of character.

The Cards, he insisted, are ready to start acting like pennant contenders; like the Mets, for example.

Red was asked if he felt his team's difficulties this season could be traced to complacency following two straight pennants, the first converted into a World Series championship.

"No, I don't think so," the St. Loo skipper replied. "They've been trying hard. They feel they can win this thing. They've been hustling. It's just that for a while we weren't able to put it all together." ■

Hallucinating —By Bill Gallo

55,862 Watch Mets Sweep, 5-1, 1-0

by Norm Miller

**O**n a beautiful afternoon in which young Gary Gentry pitched a six-hitter and the Mets slapped 13 singles to beat the Cardinals, 5-1, in a double-header opener before an SRO crowd of 55,000 at Shea yesterday, poor Ron Swoboda tied a major-league record for futility by striking out five straight times.

Jerry Koosman drew the nightcap assignment of pitching the Mets to a sweep that would keep alive their drive toward first place. Koosman was opposed by Mike Torrez, a 6-foot-6 rookie righty with a 1-3 record.

The Mets also won the second game, 1-0.

Gentry, after conceding a run in the first inning of the opener, threw blanks all the way to the ninth, when he required relief from Cal Koonce for the last two outs.

The Mets, who did not make an extra-base hit, bunched nine of their 13 singles in the third and fourth innings to score all their runs and drive out lefty Steve Carlton.

Amid the jubilation of this 17th win in the Mets' last 22 games, Swoboda suffered through his worst game in the majors. Coming to bat five times with a total of nine men on the bases, Ron whiffed four times and was called out once.

These five strikeouts tied a major league record for a nine-inning game. If it's any consolation to Swoboda, 12 players had done it before him—none of them Mets, incidentally. ■

National League Eastern Division
As of June 21

Team	Wins	Losses	Percentage	Games Back
Chicago	41	23	.641	—
METS	33	27	.550	6
Pittsburgh	34	30	.531	7
St. Louis	31	32	.402	9 1/2
Philadelphia	32	39	.451	15
Montreal	20	52	.278	27 1/2

Seaver's 11th Nips Phillies for Mets, 2-1

by Red Foley

*T*om Seaver and the Mets kept pace with the division-leading Cubs when they clipped the Phillies, 2-1, in the opener of last night's doubleheader at Shea. A crowd of about 40,000 turned out. Righties Jim McAndrew and Jerry Johnson met in the second game.

Seaver's fifth straight victory and 11th against three setbacks was the righty's 43rd lifetime, equaling the all-time high Alvin Jackson recorded during his long service with the Mets.

Seaver wound up striking out nine to run his season total to a club-leading 96.

Harrelson anchored at third as Tommie Agee rolled to short, but Cleon Jones' single to left delivered Bud with what turned out to be the winning marker. Ron Swoboda's fourth-inning single, which snapped his streak of K's at six straight, was the last of the six hits the Mets collected off Fryman.

Seaver meanwhile, wasn't having as easy a time. Except for the ninth, when he disposed of the visitors in order, they managed to get at least one runner aboard in every frame. But an alert Mets' defense took some of the load off their pitcher. ∎

DAILY NEWS

Bud Harrelson had plenty of lumber for this game against the Phillies.

june '69

Mets' Seaver Whiffs 10, Downs Pirates, 7-3

by Red Foley

 *he Mets, fortifying themselves for this week's jaunt to St. Louis and Pittsburgh, had one for the road yesterday as they downed the Pirates, 7-3, on a heady 11-hit concoction that left the 27,455 Shea customers in gay and giddy spirits.*

Tom Seaver, not at his best but plenty good enough, was the recipient of his mates' shots as he scattered six safeties and fanned 10 to chalk up his 12th victory.

Bob Veale, knocked out for the 16th straight time, was jolted for seven of the belts and all the winner's runs before staggering off in the fourth. The setback was No. 9 for the tall southpaw.

Ed Charles was one of the big celebrants as the Mets brought their four-game skid to a halt. He banged three hits and knocked in two runs. Donn Clendenon, playing first in Gil Hodges' all-right

hand-hitting lineup, chipped in with two hits and three RBIs. Cleon Jones accounted for the other markers with a two-run triple that banished Veale to the bathhouse.

Aside from some control difficulty in the early going, Seaver's major problem was Carl Taylor, Pitt's fill-in first sacker. He produced a third of the Bucs' hits and all their runs, whacking a two-run homer in the second and a three-bagger in the eighth.

Taylor's No. 2 homer melted the lead Charles and Clendenon had given Seaver with consecutive singles in the prior frame. The Mets went ahead in

National League Eastern Division

As of June 30

Team	Wins	Losses	Percentage	Games Back
Chicago	49	26	.653	—
METS	39	32	.549	8
Pittsburgh	38	37	.507	11
St. Louis	35	40	.467	14
Philadelphia	32	39	.451	15
Montreal	20	52	.278	27 1/2

the third when Charles sliced a double past Roberto Clemente's straining glove and Clendenon followed with a bounce two-bagger over third that delivered Charles and Jones, via a forcing grounder.

Seaver opened the fourth with a double and was still on second when Veale walked Tommie Agee with two out. Cleon then clouted a buzzer into left-center that skipped over Matty Alou's head to score Seaver and Agee. Bruce Dal Canton was nominated to work in place of Veale and Charles promptly greeted him with his final hit, which also delivered Jones with the Mets' final run.

Charles' spree was particularly enjoyable to the veteran. "That pinch-hit single last night and those three today should be an indication that I'm off and running," he smiled. Clendenon, who had been having trouble making contact with the ball, was ecstatic about his contribution, deciding that he, too, was "back in the groove."

Actually, Seaver's the guy who can tell them all about grooves. He has been in one for more than a month. The handsome righthander hasn't lost since the Astros clipped him, May 25, at Houston.

Since then, Tom-Tom has chalked six straight victories to equal a Met mark for such an endeavor. Yesterday's triumph, which tied him with Atlanta's Phil Niekro as the NL's top winners, also made him the winningest picther in Met history.

The victory was Seaver's 44th, one more than Alvin Jackson collected during his 5 1/2 seasons in local livery. It all adds up to some heady stuff and turned last night's jet trip to St. Louis into a champagne flight. ■

Mets pitching ace Tom Seaver (left) chats with catcher Jerry Grote.

DAILY NEWS Frank Hurley

Ron Swoboda

Ron Swoboda Learns Life Has Its Ups and Downs

by Dick Young

R on Swoboda came into the clubhouse the other day after hitting into a spectacular double play. It had taken the Mets out of the game. "I ought to go home and get my beautiful .38," he said, casually, "and blow my head off."

"Don't bother," said Rube Walker. "You'd probably miss."

The New Breed, having acquired a certain sophistication, are razzing Swoboda. He admits it's getting to him.

"I guess the booing does make me a little tight," he says. "Not that I feel hostility towards the fans. I just want so bad to change their thinking, I try too hard. I'm pressing at home."

Ron Swoboda says he plays better ball on the road, and that getting the fans off his back isn't the entire reason. "I've always wondered why a club doesn't play better ball on the road," he says. "There are less things for a player to do. I can sleep as late as I want on the road. At home there's so much to do; friends dropping in, go to the store, take care of the kids.

Ron Swoboda is an enigma. He was the first true glamour boy of Shea Stadium.

He belted 19 home runs in 1965. He wasn't ready for the majors, not really. He was a big raw talent with no finesse. Fifteen of those homers came before the All-Star break, before the pitchers took him seriously. Then they learned Ron Swoboda would chase anything, and he was done.

Swoboda would have gone to the minors, but the Mets kept him. He was an attraction, and anything that would keep the fans' mind off how pitiful the team really was, was worth keeping around.

The following year Casey Stengel was gone, and there was little else to sell. At least Ron Swoboda was a name. Again they kept him. He hit .222, and only eight homers, and they kept him. Instead of going to the minors and learning to hit, Ron Swoboda paid the price of making the Mets famous.

Now, it is a case of what-have-you-done-for-me-lately? He rides the bench, and when he gets a chance to play, he gets booed. The Mets have grown better, and Ron Swoboda has grown worse.

The other day Ron Swoboda struck out five straight times, and the fans cheered for him to make it a record six. For that moment, the perverse streak in them, the adulation of the incompetently absurd had returned.

Now, Ron Swoboda is Marv Throneberry reincarnate. He is the butt of jokes. He had one good year in 1967, before Gil Hodges managed the Mets. Ron hit .281. "I have not seen the Swoboda of 1967," says Hodges.

Perhaps he never will. Perhaps it has all passed Ron Swoboda by, which is a sad thought about a strong young man, not yet 26.

"Jim Hickman was like that," says Johnny Murphy. "He let the booing get to him. Some guys overcome it. Ed Kranepool did."

Says Gil Hodges: "I still think he has a good chance. It's going to depend on him."

Ron Swoboda is the No. 5 Met outfielder right now. Art Shamsky has pushed him out of rightfield and the first alternate has become Rod Gasper, a rookie.

Swoboda ranks himself No. 4. "I don't think I should be playing every day, not with the year Sham is having," says Ron Swoboda. "Sham is a good hitter. I always hated to see him come up against us as a pinch-hitter when the Reds had him."

Tips on Hitting

In the simplest terms, be sure you're set up there at the plate. Find a good, comfortable stance each time. There is only a split-second to decide if you'll hit or take. Be ready.

—Ron Swoboda

Capacity crowds at Shea saw their Mets beat the NL-leading
Cubs twice in a row.

July
'69

The Mets were coming on strong. But, in early July, they had to face the first-place Cubs for three games at Shea Stadium. The Mets took the first game 4-3 on a three-run rally. The second game pitted Tom Seaver against Ken Holtzman.

Seaver retired every batter he saw for eight innings. He continued his perfect game in the ninth by throwing out Randy Hundley on a surprise bunt. But, Seaver's bid for a perfect game was broken up when little-known rookie Jimmy Qualls lined to left for a single. The Mets won 4-0 on Seaver's brilliant one-hitter. It was only the fourth one-hitter in Mets history.

The Cubs rebounded from two losses to take the third game 6-2. After the game, Cub manager Leo Durocher was asked if those were the real Cubs who out-hit the Mets 10-3. "No," he barked, "those were the real Mets."

Leo "the Lip" was bolstered in his evaluation as the Mets struggled in July. The low point came when the Astros rocked the Mets for an 11-run inning in the opener and a 10-run inning in the nightcap of a doubleheader. The Mets had slipped to five games behind the Cubs and looked to be dropping further.

But, with men walking on the moon, who would count the Mets out of the race?

Tug's Marine Call Puts Strain on Met Bullpen

by Red Foley

The manager usually decides when Tug McGraw will pitch, but on Saturday, when the Mets are in Pittsburgh, Uncle Sam, rather than Gil Hodges, is going to wave the likeable lefthander out of the bullpen.

McGraw, whose rescue efforts this season have contributed to the club's unexpected rise into a bona fide contender, is slated to begin his annual two-week tour of duty with the Marines at Camp Lejune on Sunday.

It's a big 14 days for McGraw, but an even bigger fortnight for the Mets. They're booked for six games with Leo Durocher's Cubs, the first three of which will be contested beginning Tuesday afternoon at Shea.

As a result of Cpl. McGraw's military commitment, Hodges and GM Johnny Murphy huddled before tonight's Busch Stadium encounter with the Cardinals to discuss possible player manipulations they can make to replace Tug.

It won't be easy. McGraw, in addition to being a fine relief pitcher, is currently the only southpaw operating out of the Mets' pen. His presence and unique performance made Al Jackson superfluous and dictated the veteran's sale to Cincinnati last month. ■

DAILY NEWS

Tug McGraw's military commitments kept him out of the Mets bullpen. Bad weather kept McGraw's workout inside.

Those Mets! 30 Hits Maul Bucs, 11-6, 9-2

by Red Foley

If plastering nine pitchers for 30 hits is celebrating the Fourth of July with a bang, then the Mets fired a couple of shots that were heard 'round the baseball world today when they pulverized the Pirates, 11-6 and 9-2 in Pittsburgh.

In keeping with the spirit of the holiday, the Mets presented a list of heroes that in length rivaled the signers of the Declaration of Independence. Tom Seaver, Tommie Agee, Al Weis, J.C. Martin, Don Cardwell, Donn Clendenon, Art Shamsky, Bobby Pfeil and Cleon Jones were the prominent names.

Seaver and Cardwell were credited with the wins, although neither finished. Seaver, getting a late game hand from Cal Koonce, won his seventh straight in the morning opener to stretch his record to 13-3. Cardwell, a non-winner since June 6, lasted seven muggy innings in the afternoon for his third triumph. Jack DiLauro mopped up for him.

Agee and Weis, each with five hits and as many RBI, sparkled in both games, extending Pitt's losing string to six. Martin had a single and his third home run in the nightcap while Clendenon doubled home two in a four-run fifth that KO'd Bob Veale for his 10th defeat in the opener.

Shamsky, with three singles and two RBIs, was the Mets' top hit-maker in the afterpiece. Pfeil and Jones played both ends. The kid infielder helped Seaver with two hits, then punched another pair to back Cardwell's triumph. Jones, who now leads Matty Alou .353, for NL batting honors stroked four safeties in the two games.

> The customers did get a couple of thrills that weren't supplied by the Mets.

But the 17,631 customers did get a couple of thrills that weren't supplied by the visitors. Little Fred Patek and big Willie Stargell both hit homers. Patek, who looks small enough to be a jockey, jolted the tiring Cardwell for a solo that completed Pitt's scoring in the second of the finale. ∎

Mets' Smash Finish Stuns Cubs, 4-3

by Red Foley

Leo Durocher's newest bride went shopping at a Manhattan bookstore yesterday. After the Mets scored three ninth-inning runs to pull out a 4-3 Shea victory over his Cubs, the practically peerless leader of the shrinking Eastern Division leaders probably wished he'd accompanied her.

As it was, the Cubs' clubhouse was about as noisy as a library following Eddie Kranepool's game-winning hit, a looping opposite-field single that brought Cleon Jones across with the run that brought the Mets to within four games of the slumping Cubs.

Three doubles, an intentional pass, an advancing grounder and Kranepool's blooper created the frenzy for the 55,096 delirious fans (37,278 paid) and the swarm of Met benchwarmers who charged from their dugout to celebrate the victory that officially informed any doubters that this Met team is for real.

The cardiac conclusion came about with the Mets trailing, 3-1, and Ferguson Jenkins—about this far from his fourth straight victory—fashioning a one-hitter. The lone blow for eight innings was Kranepool's No. 7 homer, a shot over the right-center boards in the fifth. ∎

The Mets celebrate their 4-3 win over the Chicago Cubs at Shea.

DAILY NEWS Bill Meurer

Seaver, Perfect 8 1/3, One-Hits Cubs, 4-0

by Larry Fox

On a night that just seemed to cry out for great things, Tom Seaver and the Mets fully obliged their screaming supporters who jammed Shea Stadium to fullest capacity last night. In a World Series atmosphere, Seaver pitched a perfect game for 8 1/3 innings and ended with a one-hitter as the Mets beat the Cubs, 4-0.

It was the Mets' seventh straight victory and trimmed Chicago's first-place division advantage to three games. More importantly, the Mets are only one game back in the critical losing column and that deficit could be erased if the Mets should complete a sweep of the three-game series this afternoon.

The total crowd was 59,083, which Met vice president Jim Thomson called a record for the six-year-old ball park. Of this number, 50,709 paid, the Mets' fourth 50,000-plus crowd of the year.

Seaver struck out 11 in running his record to 14-4, with seven victories in a row. He relied mostly on his fastball and it was a fastball, ironically, that cost him the no-hitter. This was in the ninth. Randy Hundley had led off for the Cubs and bunted back to Seaver on the first pitch for the first out.

Now up came Jimmy Qualls, playing only his 18th major-league game. Qualls, a switch-hitter batting lefty against Seaver, platoons in center field with Don Young, who was the fielding goat of Tuesday's Met victory. And the youngster came up swinging. Seaver's first pitch was a fastball, out over the plate and Qualls lined it to left-center for the Cubs' first, and only, hit.

The fans, who had booed Hundley's bunt attempt, also jeered. Qualls, who said later, "I jes' closed my ears." Then the huge mob gave Seaver another encouraging ovation and Tom retired the final two batters on easy pops. ∎

Met Relapse Lets Cubs off Hook, 6-2

by Larry Fox

*ll streaks, except the continuous outpouring of fans to Shea Stadium, must come to an end. So it was yesterday as the Mets for a while reverted to their old status and lost, 6-2, to the Cubs.*

A total of 49,752 fans were in the house the city built and, of this number, 38,012 paid to put the Mets over a million with almost a half a season still to go. The total paid for the season is 1,004,472. For this three-game set with the Cubs, 163,931 made their presence heard in the ballpark and 123,999 of these were paid.

The loss stopped the Mets' winning streak at seven games and ended the division-leading Cubs' skid at five. The decision also reinstated Chicago's lead over New York to four full games, two of them in the loss column.

Now the lines are redrawn for next week's three-game return in Chicago Monday, Tuesday and Wednesday. "No, this was like any other game," winning pitcher Bill Hands declared in the boisterous Cub locker room, "but now they've got to come to rushing at us next week."

After the first two sparkling victories over the Cubs, yesterday's defeat left the taste of halvah with the Mets, but manager Gil Hodges was quick to point out that "This was a good series. Anytime you take two out of three, it has to be a good series."

However, the manager also noted that Met "mistakes" played an important role in the Cub triumph and loser Gary Gentry "didn't pitch as well as he was capable of pitching."

The Mets blew it all in a five-run fifth inning that could have been lifted right out of their Polo Grounds script. ■

There was little doubt what the Mets fans wanted as the Mets faced the Cubs.

july '69

Mets Say Gil's Great, Hawk All Wet

by Norm Miller

The Mets took a few minutes off from their pennant rush yesterday to tell Ken Harrelson he was talking through his blond mod wig when he rapped Gil Hodges. The Hawk's pop-off that Hodges was a "Jekyll and Hyde" character, the Mets agreed, was about as wild as some of the outfits he wears.

Tom Seaver, Jerry Koosman, Ron Swoboda and Ed Charles were the most indignant of the Mets players over published excerpts from a forthcoming Harrelson autobiography that he found Hodges to be "unfair, unreasonable, unfeeling, incapable of handling men, stubborn, holier-than-thou and ice-cold" when Gil was manager of the Senators.

"That doesn't seem like the manager I know," commented Seaver prior to last night's series opener against the Expos at Shea. Seaver, a well-spoken public relations student at Southern California, then jabbed the needle.

"Mr. Hodges treats his ballplayers with an attitude of professionalism," he said with exaggerated formality. "Maybe Mr. Harrelson in his immaturity couldn't tell the difference between professional treatment and someone picking on him."

Hodges, not exactly overjoyed by this distraction in the midst of the Mets' first-place push, said he had no comment to make "at this time."

Koosman saw it as a publicity stunt to promote the sale of The Hawk's book, soon to be published.

"If so, he's lost one sale on me," Kooz said. "I was shocked to read that article."

"Gil Hodges is a gentleman's gentleman," the lefty continued with feeling. "He's a wonderful person. I'm proud to play under him and know him. I'd like to be like him." ■

DAILY NEWS

Mets manager Gil Hodges

Mets, Cubs Can't Wait to Resume

by Joe Trimble

he call for revenge rang out just minutes after the final out. "Just wait until they get into our ballpark with our fans," a Cub player shouted out in the dressing room after Chicago had stopped the Mets.

It won't be long until they meet face to face again. New York opened a four-game series with Montreal last night, while the Cubs returned home for three games with Philadelphia.

After that interruption, the Cubs and Mets meet again Monday, Tuesday and Wednesday in the battle of the former winless wonders for first in the NL East.

Chicago's victory Thursday boosted the Cubs' lead over the Mets back to four games.

Both managers said they planned to use the same pitching rotation that produced fireworks at Shea Stadium this week. The Mets will use Jerry Koosman, Tom Seaver, and Gary Gentry. While the Cubs will counter with Ferguson Jenkins, Ken Holtzman and Bill Hands. ■

Ugh! Cubs Hand Tom, Mets 1-0 Zinger-oo

July 15, 1969
by Dick Young

Leo Durocher, pulling the old managerial showmanship that made him a big man to another generation, today mastered his East-leading Cubs to a 1-0 victory over Tom Seaver and the Mets. Leo, among other things, pulled his shutout pitcher, Bill Hands, with two down in the ninth and a man on first, and had Phil Regan get pitch-swinger Donn Clendenon for the final out.

It was a vengeful victory for the Cubs over Seaver, who had one-hit them in New York last Wednesday night. Seaver this time gave five hits, one less than the Mets made off Hands, but was undone by a bunt single he failed to handle in the sixth, plus a ribby single by Billy Williams.

The victory opened the Cubs' margin to 5 1/2 lengths over the Mets, but the difference on the loss side is only 3. An SRO crowd of 40,252, this on a Monday afternoon, roared to most every pitch.

Mets Rebound, 5-4; Cub Comeback Fails

by Dick Young

S *lugger Al Weis, 164 pounds of solid skin and bones, today slugged a homer, putting him only 709 behind Ruth and putting the Amazin' Mets back in the pennant race. The three-run blast, plus a circuit by Ken Boswell, enabled the Mets to stave off late solo shots back-to-back by Billy Williams and Ron Santo, and sweat it out, 5-4, over the East-leading Cubs, who now pace the Amazins by 4 1/2.*

Weis' shot was through the courtesy of Dick Selma and the U.S. Army. Selma made the mistake of grooving one with two strikes and a ball on Weis, who became the Met shortstop when Bud Harrelson went to camp for his two-week summer reservist hitch. Bud is back in a few days, but has not yet had enough practice to resume.

"Besides, Weis is doing a good job," said Gil Hodges before the game. He said it after the game, too.

The score was 1-1 going into the big moment of Al Weis' life. Both teams had scored in the third. The Met run had been delivered by Weis who had stroked a mere single and came home when Tommie Agee blasted a triple off the center wall. At least they said it was a triple. Billy Williams, covering from right when the ball caromed above the leap of Jimmy Qualls, dropped the ball trying to throw, giving Weis the extra time needed to score. ■

Up, Up and . . .   —By Bill Gallo

july '69

Mets Cut Cubs to 3 1/2 in 9-5 Slugfest

by Joe Trimble

*I*t was here in Wrigley Field, a year ago, that Gil Hodges foolishly predicted the Mets would become a pennant contender in 1970. It was here, today, that Gil Hodges conceded his Amazin' Mets have become a pennant contender in 1969.

They did it by knocking off favored Chi, 9-5, to boom to within 3 1/2 lengths of the East-leading Cubs. They did it on the homer power of Tommie Agee, Al (What, Again?) Weis and Art Shamsky, and on the gutty relief of Cal Koonce and Ron Taylor.

They did it by taking 2-of-3 from the Bruins last week at Shea, and 2-of-2 here, in the Bruin cave, under the belligerent shouts of the revived Cub fans, who turned out 36,795 again today. The six Cub-Met games, home and home, drew 236,895, and suddenly nobody is worried about the state of baseball's health.

"I think these boys have made their mark to the Cubs and to everyone else," said Hodges to newsmen in a clubhouse covered with wall-to-wall smiles. "You don't cinch a pennant in July, not with 2 1/2 months of tough baseball to play. But they certainly are a contender now. Ask any of them. They believe."

Ron Santo, captain of the Cubs, concurs. "They fooled me," he said. "They're much better than I thought they were. They're harder for us to beat than any other club." ∎

National League Eastern Division

As of July 17

Team	Wins	Losses	Percentage	Games Back
Chicago	57	36	.613	—
METS	51	37	.580	3 1/2
St. Louis	47	46	.505	10
Pittsburgh	44	47	.484	12
Philadelphia	38	50	.432	16 1/2
Montreal	28	62	.311	27 1/2

Dem Chi Bleacher Bums Ain't Foolin' Brooklyn Phil

by Dick Young

n this gotta-have-a-gimmick world, the Cubs' symbol is something called the *Bleacher Bums. They gather each afternoon in the cheap seats, wearing yellow hard hats, the kind you find on construction jobs.*

They cheer in unison, with rapid gestures, like the Rockettes. From what I can gather the Bleacher Bums are, for the most part, teenaged males, because the are stripped to the waist, for the most part.

"They are frauds," says Phil Foster. I have to believe him, because when it comes to knowing baseball fans, Phil Foster knows more than anybody in the world. He has made a living analyzing and mimicking the true baseball fan. He grew up in the Ebbets Field bleachers, and that qualifies anybody as specialist first class.

Phil Foster has just opened at the College Inn of the Palmer House here. He is playing with Barbara McNair, and next to playing with the Mets that ain't bad. Nightly, Phil Foster stands on the stage of the Palmer House and exposes Chicago's bleacher bums to the audience.

"I'll tell you why they're frauds," he says. "No self-respecting bleacher fan would submit to regimentation the way they do. Some guy stands up and says clap, and they clap. Some guy says cheer, and they cheer. That's phony. The real fan yells his own thing. He don't conform. He don't wear no yellow helmet. He's an individualist.

"The worst thing can happen to a real fan is his team gets so good that the seat to a ballgame becomes hard to get. I'll tell you why; because the real fan don't sit in the same place all game. He hasta move around. He moves over a section or two, then he yells back to his buddies. He yells, hey, you know these guys look as bad from here as they do from over there."

Another reason the Bleacher Bums are frauds, says Phil Foster, is that they came out of the woodwork when the Cubs started to imitate a big league ballclub.

"Where were they when the Cubs needed them?" demands Phil Foster. "They're front-runners: that's what they are. The true bleacher fan was there when they were losin', an' he had plenty of room to move around." ■

Docs Check Seaver's Arm

by Dick Young

Tom Seaver's million-dollar arm is due for a look-see by the Met doc soon as he gets back to New York. They don't think it's serious, but you don't take chances with property like that.

Here's how Seaver describes it: "It's a stiffness, not a pain. It's right here, under the clavicle," and he presses the front of his right shoulder. "It's not from my teeth, because I've had them looked at. It's not from sleeping on it, because I try to sleep on my left side, or on my stomach. Rube thinks it could be a cold that has settled there," meaning Rube Walker, Met pitching coach, "But I wear pajama tops to guard against air conditioning."

Here's Seaver's history of the trouble: "I first felt it the night against Chicago in New York, when I was throwing in the pen." That's the night he almost pitched a perfect game, "It worked itself out while I was warming up.

"In Chicago, next time, it didn't work itself out." He pitched nine innings, lost 1-0.

"In Montreal, it didn't work out." He was knocked out in the second.

Tom Seaver is taking butazolidin pills, and if that sounds familiar, it's the "bute" that Kentucky Derby winners aren't allowed to use. Losers, either. If it works, brace yourself for a rash of saliva-test jokes every time Seaver pitches. ■

Tom Seaver and his nephew Erick Jones join Mets owner Mrs. Joan Payson in her box before the start of the game.

DAILY NEWS Dan Farrell

How Do Mets Do It? Team Effort, Sez Gil

by Dana Mozley

With the Mets' twilight game against the Reds only an hour away, Gil Hodges yesterday was still savoring his club's come-from-behind, cliff-hanging victory the night before. "Give credit to the best team effort in the history of baseball . . . I really believe that's what this team has," he declared.

The Mets had Tom Seaver going this third game of a four-game set with Cincy. Tony Cloninger, the ex-Brave with a penchant for throwing home-run balls, was to serve for the Reds. Seaver was at 14-5; Cloninger, 7-12.

Hodges feels that his team really began to jell into a pennant contender at the time Tommie Agee earned back his regular job in centerfield. He'd been benched for light hitting on April 19 and returned on a regular basis on May 7.

"As I say, it's been a tremendous team effort," he pointed out. "But we really began to win when Tommie began to hit. It's a great thing to get that leadoff hitter on base and it's even better when he homers or starts out with an extra-base hit.

"The big difference in this team and last year's is the fact that a number of players have begun to live up to their potential. Jones was a .300 hitter in 1968; now he's a .340 hitter and an All-Star. Agee is now a strong .280 hitter, where he had to rally last last season to reach .200.

"So many of the fellows have done so much. Everyone can pick up the club, at one time or another." ∎

DAILY NEWS

Mets manager Gil Hodges looks relaxed with several of his players playing to their potential.

july '69

Seaver Throttles Reds, 3-2, for No. 15

by Dana Mozley

**T**he Amazin' Mets, who once whetted the appetites of their faithful and then failed to feed them are now serving the fans soul food. With the assistance of a great ninth-inning double play started by Rod Gaspar, Tom Seaver turned back the Reds, 3-2, at Shea yesterday to become the season's third 15-game winner.

This was Seaver's third chance to join Phil Niekro of the Braves and Denny McLain on the high plateau—one that sets all three in line to wind up with 25 triumphs. Previously, the 24-year-old Californian lost a 1-0 heartbreaker in Chicago and then, pitching with a tight shoulder, was pummeled in Montreal.

In the sixth, the Reds had to cut their deficit to one run and still had runners on first and second with none out. But Seaver recovered—to the everlasting joy of the 45,074 faithful (25,259 paid) by striking out Tony Perez, picking Chico Ruiz off second and striking out Lee May.

But, in guarding that minimum lead, Seaver saved most of the thrills for the ninth inning. That was when Bobby Tolan led off with a line single to right.

> ### Seaver was right in the midst of the two-run winning rally in the bottom of the inning.

When Perez lined low and hard toward the right-center alley, it looked like curtains—especially when Gaspar, who had just relieved Art Shamsky for defensive purposes, stumbled. But Rod, who has great speed, caught up with it and to the consternation of Tolan, who was three-quarters of the way to second, doubled up the runner at first. It was his seventh outfield assist of the season, and it was the Mets' third DP of the game.

A .100 hitter, Seaver was right in the midst of the two-run winning rally in the bottom of the inning. It all started after two out.

After Bud Harrelson singled, the pitcher doubled to right center, Harrelson stopping at third. Tommie Agee promptly joined Boswell and Ed Kranepool as co-leaders of the club's best winning RBI men—all have now won seven games—by singling through the left side for the two runs. ∎

Mets Go All Thumbs, Lose to Reds, 6-3

by Dana Mozley

O n the day when they wanted to show off for a great mass of the younger generation, the Mets yesterday should never have shown up. As 55,391 watched at Shea on helmet day—32,000 of them youngsters—the Amazin' ones brought back memories of six or seven years ago as they did everything wrong in bowing to the Reds, 6-3.

In getting no better than a half of the four-day set with Cincy, one that drew a total of 149,054 paying patrons, the Mets resembled the old-time Mets in these respects:

Making three errors, two of them by shortstop Al Weis. Getting a very poor pitching performance—one of several this year by him—from Don Cardwell.

Swinging ineffectively against a sore-armed left-hander, Gerry Arrigo, who went into the game with an earned run average of 7.20.

Falling to hustle. Alex Johnson raced for two bases when his simple "single" in the fourth inning was tardily retrieved by Tommie Agee.

Falling asleep on the bases. Donn Clendenon, who didn't realize there was only one out at the time, sprinted from first to halfway between second and third on a routine fly by Ron Swoboda in the fourth and was so far off base he was doubled up. ■

National League Eastern Division

As of July 31

Team	Wins	Losses	Percentage	Games Back
Chicago	63	41	.606	—
METS	55	43	.561	5
St. Louis	54	49	.524	8 1/2
Pittsburgh	51	50	.505	10 1/2
Philadelphia	40	58	.408	20
Montreal	33	68	.327	28 1/2

Hodges to Stand Pat on Met Pitching

by Dana Mozley

he recent ups and downs of the Mets pitching staff have manager Gil Hodges and pitching coach Rube Walker engaged in a strategic reappraisal of their mound needs for the stretch push they hope will lead to the team's first pennant.

Under the Hodges-Walker plan, starting moundsmen generally work every fifth day. There are times, however when this diagram is neither feasible nor practical, and adjustments must be made.

This happens to be one of those times. A set rotation may be desirable to Hodges, but circumstances, not necessarily under his control, preclude its function at this time.

Right now, the Mets don't have a fourth starter, or even a fifth, necessities when pitchers are working with four days between starts. Tom Seaver, Jerry Koosman and Gary Gentry, although Gary has an unhappy faculty for throwing home run balls, presently comprise Hodges' trusted starters.

Nolan Ryan, Don Cardwell and Jim McAndrew are candidates for the remaining two berths, but their credentials are not considered solid at this time. Ryan, despite a fine relief stint against the Reds on

Sunday, has been hampered with physical and military problems. McAndrew is in and out and Cardwell, despite several good efforts, is having big trouble winning.

> "I can pitch every fourth day . . . if it gets us to a point in the pennant race where you've got to pitch every fourth day, I'm all for it."
>
> —Tom Seaver

Tug McGraw has had four starts, but his relief work indicates the southpaw is of more value coming out of the pen. Ron Taylor and Cal Koonce are strictly firemen, accounting for 15 of the Mets' 22 saves. Lefty Jack DiLauro is the other pitcher. He has gone both ways but hasn't seen much action lately, appearing briefly in but two of the last 12 games.

Both Koosman and Seaver are ready and willing to alter their customary working hours.

"I can pitch every fourth day," Seaver says. "After all, if it gets us to a point in the pennant race where you've got to pitch every fourth day, I'm all for it." ■

Astros Ruin Mets Twice, 16-3, 11-5, on Big Innings

by Joe O'Day

N eil Armstrong and Buzz Aldrin walked on the moon but within the space of 10 days, another pair of astronauts—Denis Menke and Jimmy Wynn— reached Mars. The pair crashed ninth-inning grand-slam homers as the Astros landed on the Mets, 16-3, in the opener of a doubleheader yesterday at Shea Stadium before a disbelieving crowd of 22,500.

The Astros, with a 10-run 3rd inning, took the nightcap, 11-5.

Mets manager Gil Hodges then sent righthander Gary Gentry after a split, while the Astros countered with Larry Dierker.

The shots by Menke and Wynn were hardly as history-making as the combined efforts of Armstrong and Aldrin and Collins, but it was a first in the National League. Harmon Killebrew and Bob Allison of the Twins accomplished the two slams in an inning when they hit the jackpot against the Tigers in the first inning on July 28, 1962.

Relievers Cal Koonce and Ron Taylor were the victims as the Astros tallied 11 runs and busted up what threatened to be another giveaway game by the Mets, who struggled for their runs, falling behind 4-0 as early as the third inning.

Southpaw Jerry Koosman, who absorbed his sixth loss in 14 decisions, started for the Mets and quickly fell behind. Kooz didn't have his fastball popping, and the Astros jumped on his off-speed pitches for two runs in the second. ■

july '69

DAILY NEWS Dan Farrell

Yogi, Eddie, Piggy and Rube

They're Gil's Braintrust

by Dick Young

" The toughest thing to teach a kid in the big leagues today is to forget how his high school coach or college coach taught him to do it," said Yogi Berra.

"That's it," said Eddie Yost. "They come up so fast these days, they haven't had a chance to lose the habits they picked up in school. Makes it harder for guys on our level to teach. The kids have faith in the coach from school, and too often they've been taught wrong. I was lucky. My coaches in high school and college had been professional ballplayers."

"I even get it from my boy Larry," said Yogi. "I say to him why don't you sit in the middle of the plate when you're catching? He tells me his coach doesn't want him to do it that way."

They laughed. "Trouble is," said Rube Walker, "you just don't know enough about catching, Yogi."

"I remember Crosetti trying to tell a kid something," said Berra. "The kid said, my coach told me to do it the other way. Cro told him what to do with his coach!"

"I've had a young pitcher tell me to go to hell when I tried to show him something," said Joe Pignatano. "That wouldn't happen in the old days."

"I'm sitting in the stands with our Jersey scout, Pete Gebrian," said Yogi. "We're watching Montclair play Livingston. They have men on first and second, one out.

The ball is hit back to the pitcher, and he throws to third base. Pete says to me, do they do that all the time? I say, hell yes. They're afraid to throw it away at second, so they get the sure out in front. That's how they're taught."

"I wish we could teach the fans, too," said Eddie Yost. "They get on the coaches as if we're calling the strategy. If we bunt, they yell why don't you have him hit. If he hits into a double play, they say why didn't you have him bunting?"

"I get that when a man gets picked off first, too," said Yogi. "They blame me for it."

"I do," said Rube Walker. He laughed, "What some of them don't seem to realize," said Yogi seriously, "is that there's very little a coach can do. By the time he yells, the guy can be picked off. The best you can do is warn the runner when he gets to first. You say this guy has a good move. They should know that anyway, unless the kid just joined the league."

"I'll tell you one thing," said Eddie Yost. "It's nice to have crowds like we do at Shea, but it can make it tough on the coach. You can't be heard by the man at second, for all the noise. I try to move towards him, as though chasing him back, when he takes a lead and they're circling behind him."

The Met coaches get along just fine. They are of the same time, in their early and middle 40s. They eat together much of the time, and socialize. Three of them came from Washington with their leader and they adopted Yogi Berra. There is no resentment that Yogi was here first, nor that he makes more than any of them. Yogi was not shoved down Gil Hodges' throat.

"We asked Gil if he would take Yogi," Johnny Murphy has said, "and he said he'd be happy to."

"I told Gil," Berra has said, "that if he had somebody else in mind, I didn't want to stay. He said he wanted me to stay."

Berra has fitted in well. He says he is as happy now as he has ever been. "I have never felt like an outsider here," he says when you are off alone and ask him about it. "We're always talking baseball. That's what I like."

Tips on Coaching

When you take a lead off second, don't worry **about the shortstop** or second baseman. Keep **your eye on the** pitcher. He has the ball, **and as long as he has** it, nobody can tag you out. **You will learn how far** off the base you can come, **and still get back** safely from the time the **pitcher turns to** throw.

—Eddie Yost

Donn Clendenon (22) scores the winning run in the bottom of the ninth as the Mets defeat the Dodgers, 3-2.

August
'69

The Mets' slide continued from the end of July until they hit rock bottom in mid-August at nine and one half games behind the Cubs in their pursuit of the NL East title.

In the past, pennant contenders would look to the Mets for a few easy wins to bolster their record. Now the Mets were looking for a boost by beating the newly added San Diego Padres in four straight games. That got them going, and back in second place. From there, the Mets weren't looking back. They swept three games at Shea from the expatriate Dodgers.

Just to add emphasis to their return to form, Donn Clendenon punched a shot out of the park in the 10th inning to stop the San Francisco Giants' winning streak at nine games.

As August came to a close, the Mets were back in second place, three and a half games behind the Cubs and on a roll as they prepared for a crucial series against the first-place Cubs at Shea Stadium.

Astro-Naughts Leave Mets in 4-Game Slipstream, 2-0

by Phil Pepe

topper Tom Seaver was asked to put his finger in the dike yesterday and halt the flood of Astro hits and runs. You'd have to say he did a creditable job, holding hot-hitting Houston to two runs and five hits over seven innings. The only trouble is, the Mets forgot to score and dropped a 2-0 decision.

The defeat, their fourth straight and seventh in their last 11 games, gave Houston a sweep of the three-game series and dropped the Mets six games behind the Cubs, who bounced the Giants in Chicago.

For five innings, Seaver and rookie Tom Griffin were locked in a scoreless duel. Then, with two outs in the sixth, the Astros struck. The day before, the Astros had scored 11 runs in the ninth inning after two were out. This time they scored only two. It was all they needed.

Seaver fed Jimmy Wynn his 24th home run on a 3-2 pitch, which traveled over the bullpen in left. After Denis Menke lined a single to left, Curt Blefary drove one off the right-center wall. A quick, strong relay from Tommie Agee to Wayne Garrett to Jerry Grote had Menke out at home, but Grote dropped the ball for an error and the Astros had their second run. ■

National League Eastern Division
As of August 1

Team	Wins	Losses	Percentage	Games Back
Chicago	64	41	.610	—
METS	55	44	.556	6
St. Louis	55	49	.529	8 1/2
Pittsburgh	52	50	.510	10 1/2
Philadelphia	41	59	.410	20 1/2
Montreal	33	69	.324	29 1/2

Alignment Setup Backfires on Stubborn Met Bosses

by Phil Pepe

I f the Mets have fallen irrevocably out of the pennant race, they have only themselves to blame, but not for the four-game losing streak they brought into last night's game against the Braves, leaders of the NL's Wild West Show. The Mets blew it before the season.

Reportedly, Met officials balked during expansion talks last winter, reluctant to give up the Dodgers and Giants, who had accounted for one-third of the Mets' home attendance during their first seven years. They refused to go along with a strict geographical breakdown, which would have put the Mets in an Eastern Division with the Braves, Reds, Phils, Pirates and Expos.

As a compromise, Cincinnati and Atlanta went West and the Cardinals and Cubs, more appealing at the box office, joined the East.

On a strict geographical breakdown, the Mets would be right in the thick of a hot pennant race. The standings would look like this:

	Wins	Losses	Games Back
Atlanta	60	46	—
METS	55	44	1 1/2
Cincinnati	53	43	2
Pittsburgh	53	50	5 1/2
Philadelphia	42	60	16
Montreal	33	70	25 1/2

Naturally, Met officials had no way of knowing the club would be 11 games over .500 playing its 100th game. The thought was to keep the Shea turnstiles clicking, something the Mets felt the Cubs and Cardinals could do better than the Reds and Braves. But a team just a game and a half off the pace after two-thirds of the season would be its own draw.

The argument against the figures above comes from members of the Western half of the NL, who say their division is the stronger one; that the Reds and Braves would fatten up on the Expos, Phils, Pirates and Mets. The Mets can disprove the theory.

Before last night, they were 15-13 against St. Louis and Chicago, a .535 pace; against Atlanta and Cincinnati, they were 7-6, a .538 percentage. Against an Eastern Division that would include the Braves and Reds instead of the Cubs and Cardinals, the Mets would have a .565 percentage. Currently, they are playing .557 within their own group. ∎

Grote's Home Run in 11 Caps Sweep of Braves, 6-5

by Phil Pepe

Jerry Grote slammed a 2-0 pitch over the right-field fence leading off the 11th inning to bring the Mets back from a 5-0 deficit and complete a three-game sweep of the Braves at Shea Stadium yesterday.

Grote's shot, his fourth of the season, put a sudden end to the long, exciting game which the Braves seemed to have wrapped up with a four-run sixth. It made a winner of Ron Taylor and a loser of Claude Raymond and sent the Mets off on an extended road trip in a happy frame of mind. In winning, the Mets stayed six games behind the Cubs, who won their game in Chicago.

A sun-splashed crowd of 34,696 had enjoyed a five-run sixth inning outburst by the Mets, which brought them even after they had seemingly blundered the game away in the top half of the inning. The Braves also kicked in an error to equalize two by the Mets in the Braves' sixth, and the Mets added five hits to put together the tying rally.

Going into the frenetic sixth, it was a nice, uncomplicated 1-0 game, befitting the lazy, hazy summer Sunday afternoon. Catcher Bob Tillman had accounted for the only run in the third with his 10th homer, off Met rookie Gary Gentry. But in the sixth, all whatchamacallit broke loose. ∎

DAILY NEWS Frank Hurley

Met Jerry Grote is welcomed at home plate after his game-winning home run.

august '69

Reds Top Mets; Cleon Starts Again

by Phil Pepe

*O*n a night when the power-hitting Reds could score only one run, Jim Maloney pitched his strongest game in three months to defeat the Mets, 1-0, with last-out help from reliever Wayne Granger.

The Reds won, 1-0, on a two-hitter.

It was Jerry Koosman's job to try to stem the flood of Reds' hits and runs. Against the Phils yesterday, the Reds scored 19 times. The Mets didn't score that many in sweeping their last three games from the Braves. Righthander Jim Maloney started for the Reds.

Koosman kept the Red bats silent for two innings, which was some kind of moral victory. In the third, the Reds began setting off the firecrackers . . . Little ones . . . A walk to Rose, a single to right by Tolan sending Rose to third with Tolan taking second on the throw to third. Then Johnson put the Reds on the scoreboard with a sac fly to right. Koos escaped further harm by getting the dangerous Perez on a foul pop to first.

Cleon Jones chases a pop fly. He was back in action after a rest on the bench.

The Mets were unable to do much with Maloney through the first three, Garrett's double to right representing the entire offense. ∎

Mets (10-1), Reds (8-5) Swap Slugfests

by Phil Pepe

Nolan Ryan, soon to be a soldier for two weeks, and Bobby Tolan, who might make it to his Army Reserve unit in Indiantown Gap, Pennsylvania, one of these days, shared the spotlight as the Mets and Reds traded victories in tonight's doubleheader.

Ryan pitched his first complete game in more than a year by holding the hard-hitting Reds to seven hits. The Mets supported him with a 12-hit attack to take the second game, 10-1. The Reds had won the opener, 8-5, with a 12-hit attack as Tom Seaver, troubled with a stiff right shoulder, failed to go beyond the third inning.

It was difficult to tell which were the slugging Reds in the second game as the Mets exploded in an eight-run second inning, highlighted by Donn Clendenon's seventh home—a three-run shot over the left field fence, and doubles by Tommie Agee, Ed Charles and Ron Swoboda. Agee also hit his 17th homer in the fifth.

But the Reds who set off fireworks in the first game were held in check by Ryan, who reports to Fort Leonard Wood, Missouri, for two weeks active duty on Friday. ■

DAILY NEWS

Nolan Ryan (left) with Jerry Grote formed the Mets' Texas battery. The two Texans stopped the Reds in the second half of a doubleheader.

august '69

Seaver's Arm Pains Hodges

by Phil Pepe

Gil Hodges has been a Met manager long enough to have learned to take the bad news with the good. He likes the good news much better. The bad news in last night's split with the Reds (an 8-5 defeat, a 10-1 victory) was the stiffness in Tom Seaver's right shoulder and the fourth defeat in five decisions for Mr. Ace.

The good news was the return of Nolan Ryan, who put down the slugging Reds with a seven-hitter in the second game, his first victory since June 20. It was Ryan's best performance since he set a club record with 14 strikeouts against the Reds on May 14 last year. After last night's job, pitching coach Rube Walker said: "He never looked better."

The bad news about Ryan was that he was scheduled to take off this weekend for two weeks' military duty at Fort Leonard Wood, Missouri, and could not be figured on to contribute too much for the remainder of the season.

Then came the good news this morning. Ryan was informed he was not scheduled to report for duty until Monday, making him available to start Sunday's game in Atlanta, and Hodges is grateful for small favors.

As the Mets prepped for the game against the Reds here tonight, Hodges had his pitching set through the weekend—Jim McAndrew tonight, Jerry Koosman and Gary Gentry in Friday's twi-night doubleheader in Atlanta, Seaver (hopefully) Saturday night, Ryan Sunday. ■

DAILY NEWS

With Tom Seaver sore, Gil Hodges was glad to get another start out of Nolan Ryan.

august '69

Koonce Saves Seaver's 16th

Mets Nip Braves, 5-3

by Phil Pepe

Tom Seaver put his stiff right shoulder to the test tonight, but it was difficult to determine the results. It was not a Phi Beta Kappa performance for Seaver, but he did manage to pick up his 16th victory as he struggled through 7 1/3 innings, then got help from Cal Koonce for a 5-3 victory over the Braves.

After the game, Seaver admitted his arm was a little tender early, "but it worked itself out. There's no stiffness now," he added.

Manager Gil Hodges had said he would consider sending his ace righthander back to New York for further examination if the stiffness persisted, but judging from Seaver's comments, the trip will not be necessary now.

Seaver explained, "I left the game because I was tired."

Tom had pitched to 34 men, thrown 112 pitches, allowed three runs, six hits, walked five, struck out three and tossed one wild pitch when he left. The Braves had at least one baserunner in every inning except the sixth against Seaver. He seemed to be throwing more off-speed pitches than usual and to be exaggerating his follow-through.

The Mets treated Seaver to a three-run third and they needed every one of them—and more. In the Braves' third, Tom was bombed for back-to-back

Mets reliever Cal Koonce saved Seaver's 16th victory.

DAILY NEWS Walter Kelleher

home runs by Henry Aaron (his 29th this season, 539th of his career).

Seaver stayed around long enough to be a winner when the Mets scored the go-ahead run in the seventh as Cleon Jones singled Agee home. ■

Eight Years Later, Astros Still Mets' Hangup

by Phil Pepe

*I*t's a case study in child psychology. Here are twins, born eight years ago into the same impoverished, underprivileged and deprived circumstances, but placed in different environments at birth.

One goes to Texas, to oppressive heat and wide open spaces, to outdoor living and a slow and easy pace. The other is placed in the bustling, busy, cramped environment of the big city, living in New York.

The Texan grows up tough and strong; the New Yorker meek and undernourished. And whenever they meet, the Texan bullies his New York brother unmercifully. It's a case for a child psychologist.

But baseball fans will recognize the youngsters as the Mets and Astros, twins of the NL's first expansion in 1962, and while the Mets are justifiably proud of how they have matured and grown this year, they remain frustrated and embarrassed by the fact they are still getting knocked around by their Texas twin. Statistics bear out the frustration and embarrassment.

In their first seven years, the Houston kid met the New York kid 121 times and kicked the stuffing out of him 77 times. The Houston kid has been particularly viscious in his own playpen, winning 45 of the 62 games played there in the first seven years.

There is every evidence that things are getting better for the New York kid—but not against his twin. This year, they have met nine times and Houston has taken seven of them, the last six in succession. Child psychologists have a term for it. To the layman, the Mets have a hangup.

They can beat everybody else—the Big Bad Braves, the Courageous Cubs, the Rambunctious Reds, the Cruel Cardinals, even the once ferocious Dodgers and Giants—but they cannot beat the Astros, the only team to hold an edge over the Mets this season.

The Mets have won more games than the Astros and lost fewer games than the Astros, but when they meet on the same field, it is as if Joe Frazier is in the ring with Tiny Tim. There is no logical explanation for it. No good reason, no answer. It just happens. And it's getting frustrating. ■

> The Mets have won more games than the Astros, but when they meet on the same field, it is as if Joe Frazier is in the ring with Tiny Tim.

August '69

Astros, Griffin Extend Hex Over Mets, 3-0

by Phil Pepe

I f the Astrodome is the eighth wonder of the world, as the Astro scoreboard modestly proclaims, then the Astros' rookie righthander, Tom Griffin, is easily the ninth wonder of the world at least.

The Mets would give Griffin top billing over the Dome as a tourist attraction they could do without. Griffin pitched his usual scoreless ball against the Mets tonight, getting credit for the 3-0 victory with his usual ninth-inning help from Fred Gladding. It's getting to be a joke what Griffin is doing to the Mets.

He has now pitched 25 innings against them and the Mets still have not scored a run against him. He has allowed them just 13 hits (four tonight) and struck out 28 of them (nine tonight, four of them named Bobby Pfeil).

Against the Mets, Tom Griffin looks like Walter Johnson. Against everybody else, he looks like Howard Johnson. Tonight's victory was Tom Griffin's eighth, but take away the Mets and he's just another promising young pitcher with one shutout (over San Diego), an ERA over four per game and a record of 5-5. The Mets are keeping him in the league. ■

Mets manager Gil Hodges still hasn't figured out the Houston Astros, his Mets losing nine straight to their Texas Twin.

august '69

Mets Lose Ninth Straight to Astros 8-2

by Phil Pepe

he Mets finally found a reason to celebrate in Texas. They left the Astro-dome. They will not be back here again until next year.

Singing, "We hate to see you go," the Astros bid farewell to their New York visitors with an 8-2 victory tonight. They rubbed the Mets' noses in Astroturf. It was the ninth straight time the Astros had defeated the Mets this year, their 10th victory in the 12 games played between the two clubs and completed a clean sweep of the six games in the Dome.

It was only the third time in Mets history that they were shut out in the park. They failed to win in Crosley Field, Cincinnati, in 1962 and they did not win in Milwaukee County Stadium in 1965. Both of those blankings came when the Mets played each club in the league nine times and it may be significant that they don't go back to County Stadium anymore and Crosley Field will soon be dismantled. The

Astrodome, unfortunately, is here to stay.

Gentry started for the Mets, his sixth try at victory No. 10. He has not won since July 15. His trouble, Gentry says, is that sooner or later he has one bad inning that beats him. Tonight his bad inning came sooner. It couldn't have come any sooner.

He retired the leadoff batter, Jesus Alou, then went into a slump. He hit Joe Morgan, then walked Jimmy Wynn after Morgan stole second. He got Norm Miller to hit to second, a perfect double play ball. But Ken Boswell had trouble getting the ball out of his glove and could get only the force at second.

Gentry should have been sitting in the Mets' dugout; instead he was pitching to Denis Menke with two out and runners on first and third. ■

Mets Finally Set Casey "Free"

August 14, 1969
by Dick Young

Casey Stengel is off the Mets' payroll. He reveals he got $50,000 for his first year of retirement, 25 for the next and 12 1/2 for the last. That ended the arrangement. Casey now represents the club for love. "They were very good to me," he says. And vice-versa.

As Gil Was Saying, His Goal Is to Win 85

by Phil Pepe

f the joyride is over for the Mets, history will record that it ended in Houston, where men prepare to take off for the heavens and Mets come down to earth.

Nobody really expected it to last very long, anyway. The Mets spent 72 days in the high rent district of the National League's posh East Side. That's 72 days in second place. That's something.

The Mets have dropped below the Cardinals, have fallen 9 1/2 games behind the Cubs, eight on the losing side, and suddenly find themselves in a battle to hold off the Pirates to save third place. All the hysteria of July, all the tumult and wild dreams that the Mets could do the impossible and win, of all things, a division championship, are gone.

But perhaps that's losing sight of the real issue, the primary objective. In the spring, Gil Hodges set a goal. It was a modest goal. The goal was to win 85 games. It is still reachable. ■

Met Tommie Agee (20) is greeted by teammates after hitting a game-winning home run against the Giants.

Mets Look to Padres as Pick-Me-Up

by Phil Pepe

For years pennant winners and contenders fattened up on the Mets. Now it's the Mets' turn to pick on the underprivileged. In need of a pick-me-up after their worst road trip since 1967, the Mets will have a chance to take it out on one of their patsies, the expansion San Diego Padres, in a four-game weekend series.

It couldn't come at a better time. After winning four out of eight against the Reds and Braves, the Mets ended the trip by getting kicked three times in the Astrodome by the surging Astros.

The Mets find themselves in third place, 9 1/2 games off the pace, one game back of the second-place Cardinals and a shaky 3 1/2 ahead of the fourth-place Pirates. The Padres may be just what the Mets need to find peace of mind. ■

Tale of 2 Cities:
NL up, AL down in Chicago, New York
August 17, 1969
by Joe Trimble

Baseball runs in cycles. Now it is the NL's turn to dominate in the only two-team cities in the majors, New York and here. Chicago is divided into the North Side and the South Side (as they border Lake Michigan) and, of course, one can go West. However, you can't go very far East unless you want to get your feet wet.

So it is the Cubs on the North Side who own the town, similar to New York, where the Mets have become No. 1 after all those years of Yankee domination.

It didn't take long for the turnabout to come in either city. Just two years ago, the White Sox were battling for the pennant in the four-way race which finally ended with Boston's "Impossible Dream." The Sox lasted until the middle of the last week when they dropped a twi-nighter to Kansas City (now Oakland).

At that time, the papers here carried fan letters demeaning the Cubs and criticizing owner Phil Wrigley. All was praise for the Sox. Now it is the other way. Leo is the Lion and Ernie Banks is the sweetest on this side of heaven.

While the Cubs have been soaring for the NL East title and perhaps their first one since 1945, the Sox have been falling down. They are in the AL West cellar behind the two new expansion clubs, Seattle and Kansas City.

Now the papers and fans exult in every move by the Cubs and the letters from the customers tell owner Arthur Allyn to take his pale hose out of town…and Milwaukee isn't far enough.

A few years ago, a weekend series with the Yanks here would exceed 125,000 in attendance. The current series of four single games (three nights and Sunday) will attract barely 40,000.

Mets Return to Second;

2-0, 2-1, No. 17 for Seaver

by Phil Pepe

After spending two days in third place in the NL East, the Mets decided they didn't like the neighborhood. So they broke the lease yesterday, picking on the poor, underprivileged Padres for 2-0 and 2-1 victories that pushed the Mets back into second place by two percentage points over the Cardinals.

Tom Seaver won his 17th in the first game, but left after eight innings complaining of tenderness in his right shoulder again. Ron Taylor pitched the ninth. Jim McAndrew picked up the win in the second, with help from Tug McGraw, as the Mets dazzled the Padres with their arms, if not with their bats.

Seaver's game is of prime importance, for statistical and physical significance. The victory made him the first 17-game winner in the National League, beating the Cubs' Ferguson Jenkins to that distinction by three hours. It was also his high as a Met—he won 16 in each of his last two seasons—and a record for a Met right-hander.

"I started to get tired in the eighth," he said, "and I felt some tenderness (in the shoulder). Rube (pitching coach Walker) saw it, too. When I came to the bench, he said, 'I think you've had it.' I told him 'I was just going to tell you the same thing.'" ∎

National League Eastern Division

As of August 17

Team	Wins	Losses	Percentage	Games Back
Chicago	74	44	.627	—
METS	64	51	.557	8 1/2
St. Louis	66	53	.555	8 1/2
Pittsburgh	60	56	.517	13
Philadelphia	48	69	.410	25 1/2
Montreal	38	81	.319	36 1/2

A Banner Day: Mets 3-2 San Diego Twice

by Phil Pepe

When the last of the 3,612 banners had paraded past home plate at Shea yesterday, 12 Mets dashed out to the left side of the infield, each carrying a huge card. When the cards were held aloft, they spelled out "You Turn Us On!"

The Mets were not exactly burning with both jets open yesterday, but they were turned on just enough to sweep a double-header, 3-2 and 3-2, from the Padres. And if that's what a banner day crowd of 35,711 can do, there should be 81 banner days in Shea.

Yesterday the Mets came to bat in 16 innings and scored in only two of them, which may be considered a tribute to the Padres' arms or the Mets' bats. In any case, the Mets made them both three-run innings and that was all they needed.

It was all very reminiscent of six and seven years ago. Only the outcome was reversed. It used to be you could stay close to the Mets and sooner or later you'd get the two or three runs that would beat them. The Mets used that formula on the expansion Padres yesterday. They were able to do it because they had excellent pitching from Jerry Koosman, Don Cardwell and Ron Taylor.

The Mets scored 10 runs in the back-to-back doubleheaders Saturday and yesterday, but held the Padres to five runs to sweep the four games and go 15 games ahead of .500, their highest point in history. ■

DAILY NEWS Frank Hurley

The Mets' Cleon Jones makes a somersaulting catch to help the Mets sweep the Padres.

Swoboda Sweeps Bases, Dodgers in 7-4 Win

by Phil Pepe

Suddenly rejuvenated Ron Swoboda cracked a bases-loaded double that cleared the bases and sparked a four-run seventh inning to give the Mets a come-from-behind 7-4 victory and a sweep of the three-game series over the Dodgers before 48,435 delighted Metniks at Shea yesterday.

The victory gave the Mets nine out of 10 on the home stand and a 21-5 record against the three California teams. It also assured them of the season edge on the Dodgers as they won their seveth in nine games against LA, sweeping all six games at Shea. They have three left with the Dodgers in LA.

Cleon Jones started the winning rally, opening the seventh with his third hit, a single to left. Art Shamsky followed with his second hit, and Ken Boswell was credited with a hit when reliever Jim Brewer fielded his bunt and threw too late to third to get Jones.

Swoboda then hit Brewer's 1-0 pitch for his base-clearing double to left, and Jerry Grote drove in the fourth run with his third hit of the game and sixth in two games, a single to center.

The rally made a winner of Cal Koonce, the Mets' third pitcher, who picked up his sixth straight victory after dropping his first three decisions this season.

The Mets started out as if they would make short work of Sutton. Singles by Pfeil and Jones and Boswell's wallop jammed the sacks with two out and Swoboda batting. This time Rocky delivered without swinging, getting his usual bases-loaded walk to force in a run. Second baseman Sizemore took Grote's soft liner to leave three Mets stranded. ∎

DAILY NEWS Frank Hurley

The Mets' Ron Swoboda gets under the tag at third. He didn't work as hard when he walked in a run against the Dodgers.

Even Lip's Poodle Couldn't Save San Deigo

by Dick Young

hat Leo Durocher. He'll go to any lengths to stop the Mets. Last night he had one of his secret agents release a frisky French poodle onto the playing field here, but that stopped the Amazins for only five minutes; then they went right about the business at hand, which was thrashing the San Diego Patsies, 8-4 and 3-0.

This put the Mets hot on the heels of Durocher and his Cubs, and he'll have to think of something else now. The double dip put the Mets as close to a pennant as they've ever been. Just three lengths from the top; one notch off on the loss side.

The collar on the pooch wasn't as tight as the one throttling the Cubs, who lost again today and are now 2 1/2 up, all on the win side.

After all, a French poodle is no match for Tom Seaver and Jim McAndrew, or for Clendenon, and Swoboda, and Cleon, and Shamsky. Seaver, working his first CG in a month, held the Padres to five hits in the first, and McAndrew gave them five in the second. Clendenon and Swoboda hit homers in the first and Jones banged a 2-ribby double for the lead runs. Al Weis and Shamsky stroked timely singles in the second game. ∎

Now Even Hodges Forced to Admit It: Mets a Contender

August 27, 1969
by Phil Pepe

It wasn't exactly a threat, a promise or a Joe Namath guarantee, but it was the closest thing to an admission Gil Hodges has uttered in a year and three-quarters as manager of the Mets. He had just swept the Dodgers, concluding a 9-1 home stand and inching closer to the top, when the manager of the Mets was asked if he considered his club a contender.

"Where have you been?" Hodges questioned the questioner. "Yes, we're a contender."

Where the questioner had been was noting that in the spring, Hodges said his goal was 85 victories this year, hardly enough to put him in a contending position.

"I might have to change it when we get to 85," Hodges said the other day.

"It's too early," the manager of the Mets kept saying. "If we're this close by September, then I'll consider us a contender."

Evidently, the manager figures September is close enough and so is first place, so the time has come for everyone—Hodges included—to take the Mets seriously.

Met Home Run in 10th Ends Giant streak at 9, 3-2

by Dick Young

The Amazin' Mets today broke the Giants' nine-game winning streak in a most amazin' several ways, most of them by Donn Clendenon. Donn, in the game only because Cleon Jones had a day off to rest his sore hand, blasted the 10th-inning homer that beat Gaylord Perry, 3-2. Donn also picked up a couple of loose balls to make screwy double plays in the eighth and ninth, throwing one man out at the plate and another at third.

Defensive outfielder Rod Gaspar also cut down a decisive run at the plate with a spectacular peg in the ninth, as the Mets mixed misplays and superplays in a dazzling concoction for the 14,436 fans.

The Mets got a run off Perry in the second with some help from Gaylord's supporting cast. Boswell, who had led with a single to center, took second on a passed ball by Dietz. One out later, Grote bounced to short. Boswell, with a good lead, beat the peg to third and both were safe. Harrelson then singled up the middle for the run. Perry shut it off there by fanning Cardwell and getting Agee on a grounder.

There followed some weird scorelessness as both teams blew chances to end the game in regulation time. The Mets in the top of the ninth had a man on third with one down as Swoboda doubled to right and was bunted along by Grote. Here, with Cleon Jones swinging for Harrelson, the Giant infield came in. Jones chopped one to the mound. Perry, with a leap, deflected it to shortstop Lanier, who feigned the runner back and pegged to first. Lanier also threw out J.C. Martin, swinging for the pitcher.

The pitcher was Ron Taylor, who had come in in the eighth with the bases full and one down. A walk, Lanier's bloop hit to center to end a 17-for-0 slump, and Boswell's boot of a DP ball had created the jam. Mason then popped down the right line. Boz took it as pinch-runner Henderson tagged and broke.

Henderson came halfway and started back. Boz fired home. The ball struck first base coach West Westrum on the arm and dribbled onto the infield. Clendenon recovered it as Henderson again broke for home. ∎

> There followed some weird scorelessness as both teams blew chances to end the game in regulation time.

National League Eastern Division

As of August 31

Team	Wins	Losses	Percentage	Games Back
Chicago	81	52	.609	—
METS	75	53	.586	3 1/2
St. Louis	71	60	.542	9
Pittsburgh	69	59	.539	9 1/2
Philadelphia	52	76	.406	26 1/2
Montreal	40	92	.303	40 1/2

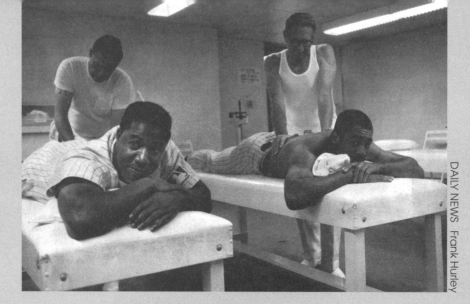

DAILY NEWS Frank Hurley

Tommie Agee

Mess to Marvel in a Year, Tom Agee Has Arrived

by Dick Young

One day last season, when Tommie Agee was batting, the pitcher threw over to first and Agee almost swung at it. "I was just messed up all year," says Tommie Agee.

The fact that Tommie Agee played in 132 games in 1968 is either a tribute to his indomitable determination, or evidence of what little choice the manager had. Probably some of both.

Very likely, there wasn't a worse hitter in the league last year than Tommie Agee. He needed a blazing finish to bat .217. At one stage, he was going 0-for-April. Then he lashed a single up the middle, and the people in Shea Stadium arose and cheered him. It was not the cheer of sarcasm you hear so often in ballparks. This was genuine elation from the fans, a show of appreciation that he had hung in there to snap his oppressive run of 34 consecutive outs.

Tommie Agee has made it, and everybody on the club feels good for him. He wouldn't quit on them, and he wouldn't quit on himself. A pro admires that above all.

"He was just all messed up last year," says Cleon Jones, who knows him better than anyone. "He got off bad and couldn't get himself together."

The first time up, in the opening Met exhibition game, Tommie Agee was hit on the head by Bob Gibson. That's getting off about as bad as you can.

"That bothered him all season," says Johnny Murphy. "I'm sure of it. He was in a strange league, in addition. He got so mentally whipped he couldn't do a thing."

But Tommie Agee kept doing his thing in centerfield, and that's what Tom Seaver and the rest admired about him.

Tommie Agee has made money right from the start. He was signed to a $65,000 bonus contract by Cleveland in '61. It took him five years to make the majors, but when he did he was rookie of the year, and by that time he had been traded to Chicago. The Mets got him in December, 1967, by giving Tommy Davis.

Tommie Agee and Cleon Jones kid about their childhood together in Mobile, and how hard things were.

"We'll be at a gathering," says Tommie Agee, "and Cleon will remember how he came to my house to ask for something to eat, and he was so weak he could hardly knock on the door. And he says that when he did, I was so weak I couldn't open it."

Tommie Agee laughs. "It wasn't really that bad," he says. "In fact, we were pretty well taken care of. But it's much better now."

Hank Aaron was asked to compare Tommie Agee and Cleon Jones. "Cleon may be a little better hitter than Tommie," he said. "He has more control of the bat. Both are powerful, but Tommie will hit more home runs. He has that type of swing. Cleon will go with the pitch more.

"Agee," added Hank Aaron, "is as good a centerfielder as you'll see in the league right now. The more he plays in this league, the better he'll become. He doesn't know all the hitters yet, but he makes up for it with his speed.

"Cleon is a bit more temperamental. He'll let things get under his skin more than Tommie does. But he certainly has come a long way, and will get better. Both of them will."

Tips on Pitching

Learn the fundamentals, but always have an attitude to win. Remember, you're not going to get hits all the time. When you don't, ask yourself "What can I do to help my club? How can I get the man on second over to third base? What can I do on defense? It's your team. You have to contribute something.

—Tommie Agee

Tommie Agee (20) and Bud Harrelson (3) welcome home Donn Clendenon after he hit the home run that clinched the NL East for the Mets.

September '69

The Mets were on a roll.

Tom Seaver became the Mets' first 20-game winner on September 5, 1969, with a five-hit win over the Phillies.

With the NL East title on the line in two games against the Cubs, the beanballs were flying. Jerry Koosman struck out 13 Cubs in the series opener. Ron Santo, one of the few Cubs to avoid being struck out, was struck on the right arm with a pitch. Koosman was watching out for his own after Bill Hands knocked down Tommie Agee.

Agee ended up being the difference when he cracked a two-run homer and scored the winning run in a 3-2 battle.

The second game of the series was never in doubt, as the Mets thrashed the Cubs 7-1, leaving the Mets only a half-game out of first place.

Just 24 hours after the Cubs slunk out of town, the Mets claimed first place by winning the first half of a doubleheader with the Expos in extra innings. After Nolan Ryan claimed his sixth win of the season in the nightcap, the Mets were a full game up on the Cubs.

For once, the Mets could do no wrong. Even as the Mets struck out 19 times against Steve Carlton, they still found a way to beat the Cardinals in a game on the road.

Once they had the division lead, the Mets weren't going to give it up. They clinched the division on September 24 in front of a packed Shea Stadium. Gary Gentry shut out the Cardinals for a 6-0 win and the first ever National League East title.

Mets Ax Giants, 8-0; Seaver's 19th

by Dick Young

The Amazin' Mets, bombing away behind their ace, ripped the Giants, pride of the West, 8-0, in today's opener, tentatively knocking them out of first place in their section. For Tom Seaver, it was win No. 19, matching the Met high set last season by Jerry Koosman.

Seaver had a couple of apprehensive moments for an easy win. One came when a sailing fastball hit Ron Hunt in the rear of the helmet. The other came when reliever Bob Bolin decided to knock down Seaver, and nipped him on the left arm with the pitch.

The Mets bombed out Mike McCormick in the five-run fifth, slapped slightly at Herbel, then banged Bob Bolin for three more in the fifth. That put the Mets in a rather enviable position, with an 8-0 lead, with Seaver pitching.

Walks to Agee and Clendenon, sandwiching Jones' hit through short, filled the bases for Swoboda, who sliced a two-ribby double into the right corner, past Henderson's dive.

Grote singled in two more and, with one down, Seaver hit through the left side off Herbel to make it

five. Confident enough to give Jones' sore hand the remainder of the game off, Hodges put Gaspar in for Cleon to open the fifth, and Rod opened the next fuss with a hit to left-center.

Seaver survived two crises. The first two men got on in the second, and the bags were left loaded in the third. McCovey the Menace opened the second with a triple down the center-left slot in the overshift. Seaver then carefully walked Bonds, fanned Marshall, bent a changeup curve past Hiatt's stare, and slipped a pop-pill to Lanier. It was quite scientific.

Next stanza, a single, hit batsman and walk to McCovey filled the bags with two down. Bonds then skied out. ■

National League Eastern Division

As of September 1

Team	Wins	Losses	Percentage	Games Back
Chicago	82	52	.612	—
METS	76	53	.589	3 1/2
Pittsburgh	70	60	.538	10
St. Louis	71	62	.534	10 1/2
Philadelphia	52	78	.400	28
Montreal	40	92	.303	41

september '69

Donn's Dandy Bat Boosts Met Morale

by Red Foley

T*he Mets winged home from California yesterday knowing that Donn Clendenon's home-run hitting, like his trumpet playing, won't relegate either Babe Ruth or Harry James to respective anonymity.*

But they really didn't care because Clendenon, with five homers, eight ribbies and a .393 batting average, had some kind of tour. Dr. Timothy Leary should have such a trip. In fact, if the rest of the Mets had done half as well as Clendenon, they wouldn't be entering tonight's Shea pair with Philly 5 1/2 games behind the division-leading Cubs.

The Mets won six of 10 during the Coast expedition, a sojourn that may have earned the 34-year-old Clendenon permanent possession of first base. Since coming here from Montreal in June, he has been platooning with Ed Kranepool in Gil Hodges' lefty-righty rigmarole.

Now, with Kranepool still idled by the hand he bruised three weeks ago in Houston, Hodges undoubtedly will stick with Clendenon. Art Shamsky and J.C. Martin have played first to conform with the manager's strategies, but the way Clendenon has been socking the ball during his current seven-game hitting streak would dictate his retention against both types of pitching. ■

Young Ideas
September 7, 1969
by Dick Young

Have you wondered how the two ajor leagues would look if the Lords Baseball hadn't gone for divisional ay? This is how. Color it ridiculous: These standings are compiled as of mes played Wednesday, September 3, date both leagues concluded inter-isional play for the season. There s been no appreciable change.)

National					American				
Team	Win	Loss	Pct.	G.B.	Team	Win	Loss	Pct.	G.B.
Cubs	84	53	.613	—	Orioles	92	44	.676	—
METS	77	56	.597	5	Twins	82	52	.612	9
Giants	76	59	.563	7	Tigers	79	56	.585	12 1/2
Dodgers	74	59	.556	8	Athletics	75	58	.561	15 1/2
Reds	73	59	.553	8 1/2	Red Sox	72	62	.537	19
Braves	74	63	.540	10	Senators	71	66	.518	21 1/2
Pirates	71	61	.538	10 1/2	Yankees	67	67	.500	24
Cardinals	72	63	.533	11	Angels	56	76	.424	33
Astros	70	64	.522	12 1/2	Royals	54	80	.403	37
Phillies	54	79	.406	28	White Sox	53	79	.402	37
Padres	40	95	.295	43	Indians	54	82	.397	38
Expos	41	95	.301	42 1/2	Pilots	50	83	.376	40 1/2

Seaver Wins 20th, 5-1, Then Mets Fall, 4-2

by Red Foley

hen Tom Seaver won the game he wanted and the Mets lost the one they needed, last night's Shea twinner became a split with Philly that left the locals 4 1/2 games behind the division-leading Cubs.

Seaver became the first 20-game winner in Met history as he five-hitted the Phillies, 5-1, in the twilight segment. That victory, blended with the Pirates' matinee win in Chicago, narrowed the gap to four games, two on the vital losing side.

Seaver's victory, which also made him the first 20-gamer in the National League this season, was a dandy. He walked only one and fanned seven. Three of Philly's hits, although they weren't gifts, could be attributed to the condition of an outfield that had been turned into a squishy bog by the recent rains.

Philly had no such alibi when the Mets scored three times in their half. That's because the locals, scoring two unearned runs, didn't get the ball out of the infield. There was one out and Swoboda aboard via a pass when the Mets struck.

Jerry Grote rapped to the right side, and what might have become a 3-6-3 doubleplay wound up with Mets at the corners when Richie Allen failed to come up with the bouncer. When Grant Jackson, whose 5-0 lifetime mark vs. the Mets was to go down the drain, walked Rod Gaspar, the sacks were stuffed.

Al Weis then hit a skipper over the mound. It looked like an inning-ending DP ball until Jackson deflected it. He slowed the ball just enough for Weis to get an infield hit as Swoboda crossed.

Seaver then smacked what might have been another inning-ending grounder to Cookie Rojas.

The second baseman's throw to Don Money forced Weis as Grote scored the go-ahead marker. When Money got tangled up on Weis' takeout try, he refrained from throwing to first.

Asked if he'd treasure the ball with which he fanned Alex Johnson for the final out, Seaver said he would, "Right now, I've got a few baseballs from what I consider important games, but I haven't got them really displayed. In fact, I'm keeping them in an old sock until the day my wife and I move into a permanent home." ■

> "Right now, I've got a few baseballs from what I consider important games . . . I'm keeping them in a old sock until the day my wife and I move into a permanent home."
>
> —Tom Seaver

Tom Seaver

om Seaver's selection was the turning point in the dramatically changed fortunes for the Mets, and it came by a quirk of fate. Tom was originally signed by the Braves but William D. Eckert, then commissioner, voided the deal, ruling the club had violated the agreement not to sign a player whose college season had started. The USC star became a free agent. His name was placed in a hat and it was drawn by the Mets. He won 16 in 1967 when he was the NL Rookie of the Year, and again in 1968. His 22 wins to date this year are tops in the NL and give him the honor of being the first Met in the 20-game circle. The strong righty, whose dad was a Walker Cup golfer, will be 25 in November. Tom's wife Nancy, a beautiful blonde, nervously twists a hanky when Tom wheels and deals.

Jerry Koosman

A Shea Stadium usher and the U.S. Army are responsible for giving the Mets Jerry Koosman, hailed as "the new Koufax." The usher's son was catching for the Fort Bliss team and wrote his dad, raving about a fireballing lefty from Appleton, Minn. Dad tipped off the Mets. They scouted the lefty in Texas, liked what they saw and signed him in 1964. As a rookie last year, Kooz set a club record with 19 victories, a 2.08 ERA and seven shutouts. The shutouts tied a league mark for a rookie. Named to the All-Star Team, Koosman came in to fan Carl Yastrzemski for the last out and nailed down the 1-0 NL victory. Kooz is 25, 6-foot-2, 200 pounds.

Cleon Jones

C leon Jones was destined to be a star. He comes from Mobile, Ala., which produced Willie McCovey, Hank Aaron, Billy Williams and Tommie Agee, Cleon's roommate and buddy. Agee and Jones played on a high school team that lost one game in three years, but football was Cleon's game. He set a state record with 26 TDs one season and won a scholarship to Alabama A&M, but gave up football to sign with the Mets in 1962. Jones batted .275 as a rookie in 1966, slumped to .246 the following year, but really arrived last year when his .297 BA was sixth best in the NL. Now he is in a position to become the Mets' first bat champ.

Tommie Agee

Tommie Agee with Cleon Jones form the Mets' Mobile Unit. They grew up together in Mobile, Ala., and now are roomies and neighbors in the Mets' outfield. Agee's Pygmalion transformation is a major factor in the club's surge. AL rookie of the year for the White Sox in 1966, he was obtained before the '68 season to plug the Met's centerfield gap. He bombed, with a .217 BA, five HRs, 17 RBI. This year, magic. Agee is high on the club list in almost every offensive department and has a shot at the Met record for homers, 34. Tommie, due for a raise and a possible Series cut, is 27 and single. He has it made.

Ron Swoboda

Ron Swoboda, called Rocky by his teammates, is the enigma of the Mets. Signed in 1963 out of Baltimore (Babe Ruth's home town, the Mets noted hopefully), he was the strong boy who would lead the Mets out of oblivion. As a rookie in 1965, he hit 19 homers, more than Mickey Mantle, Roger Maris or Stan Musial hit as rookies. But he batted .222. His .281 in 1967 was encouraging. His .241 last year was not. He led the club in RBI with 59 in 1968; also in Ks with 113. At 6-foot-2, 205 pounds and only 25, there is still hope Ron will be a big NL star.

Edward Kranepool

E d Kranepool knows better than most the rags-to-riches story of the Mets. He has lived it. From the frustration of '62 to the joy of '69. He was signed out of Monroe High in the Bronx, alma mater of Hank Greenberg, for 85G in '62 and played in three games with the original Mets at age 17, and has played on every Met club since. Ed came up to stay in '64 and was the Mets' representative in the 1965 All-Star Game. He shares the club record for homers by a lefty-hitter with Marv Throneberry, 16 in '66, and his 62 career homers is a Met mark. Kranepool, an eight-year vet at 24, is a stockbroker in the off-season.

Nolan Ryan

N olan Ryan is the hardest thrower among the hard-throwing Met pitchers. Injuries and service commitments prevented him from winning more than six games this year, but his promise showed with a better strikeout-per-inning ratio. Selected in the fifth round of the '65 free-agent draft. Nolan won 17 games the following year for Greenville, Williamsport and Mets. Ryan set a Met record by fanning 14 in one game vs. Reds last May. His fast ball has been dubbed the "Ryan Express." A 6-foot-2, 195-pound righthander, the 22-year-old Ryan lives in Alvin, Texas.

Jerry Grote

B esides trouble, the only thing the Mets ever got from the Astros is Jerry Grote, who came in one of those obscure minor league deals. Grote was with the Astros' Oklahoma City farm when the Mets got him for pitcher Tom Parson (who?) after the 1965 season. Jerrry caused no tremors his first two seasons as a Met, batting. 237 and .195. Last year, he became the club's first-string catcher and an All-Star starter as he batted an impressive .282. The tough Texan who will be 27 next month, has one of the best arms in the NL, and super thief Lou Brock calls him "the toughest catcher in the league to steal against."

September 8

Mets Roll, 9-3; Bring on the Cubs!

by Red Foley

The Mets, who knocked out a Champion when they slugged the Phillies, 9-3, yesterday, challenge a would-be title holder at Shea Stadium tonight. Chicago's collapsing Cubs, their once-fat bulge melted to 2 1/2 games, arrive for a two-night reception the aroused Mets gave Billy Champion and his Philly playmates.

It took a two-run seventh and a four-run eighth to turn this one into a laugher, but it wasn't until the locals broke a 3-3 knot that the Mets or the 28,927 excited payers could do any heehawing.

While all this was going on, the Shea scoreboard was flashing the doings from Wrigley Field. The Flushing patrons were voicing their approval as Pitt maintained its lead.

At least, the Pirates were holding an edge. The Mets had gotten a lead in the first inning when Tommie Agee and Art Shamsky slammed homers for a 2-1 lead.

But that dissolved quickly when Philly poked starter Gary Gentry for two in the fifth to move in front, 3-2. The visitors had nicked Gentry for a go-ahead run in the lead inning when Tony Taylor doubled and Rich Allen followed with a single. ∎

DAILY NEWS   Dan Farrell

Tommie Agee slides into home past the tag by Chicago catcher Randy Hundley in the first of two games at Shea Stadium. Hundley was sure he had the tag, and jumped up and down when the umpire called Agee safe.

Kooz Ks Kubs, 3-2; Mets 1 1/2 Back

Agee HRs for 2, Scores Icer

by Red Foley

Jerry Koosman, with assists from Tommie Agee, Wayne Garrett and an enterprising photographer, pitched the Mets to within 1 1/2 games of first place last night when he fanned 13 Cubs in a 3-2 Shea win that left 48,930 rain-soaked onlookers chanting "we're number one."

"I looked at some sequence photos a fellow made of me pitching recently and saw what I was doing wrong," the happy Koosman said in the Met clubhouse. "The pictures showed I wasn't getting my body and my arm working the right way and that's why I wasn't getting too many strikeouts."

Koos got them last night, nailing every Cub but Don Kessinger and Ron Santo at least once. Kooz also nailed Santo, but it was with a swifty that slammed into the third baseman's right arm while he was batting in the second inning.

It could have been repayment for the duster loser Bill Hands decked Agee with when he was leading off in the Mets' first. If this is so, it might lead to some fancy ducking by both sides when the Mini-Pennant Series resumes with Tom Seaver serving against Kenny Holtzman tonight.

The Mets led, 3-2, after six innings, cutting a 2-2 knot the visitors had tied in the sixth. Agee's double and Garrett's following single produced the go-ahead marker—but not without a fuss. Both Cub skipper Leo Durocher and catcher Randy Hundley beefed loud and long after plate ump Dave Davidson ruled Agee had beaten right-fielder Billy Williams' toss to the plate on Garrett's single. It was a bang-bang play at home.

Agee, whose No. 26 homer—following Bud Harrelson's single in the third—had given the Mets a 2-0 edge, led off the fatal sixth with a shot past Santo into left. It started out as a single but became a two-bagger when Agee, realizing Billy Williams would have trouble fielding the hit in the sodden grass, stretched it into a double. ∎

Hard-throwing Jerry Koosman fires away at the Cubs. Koosman struck out 13 Cubs, including three in the ninth inning.

DAILY NEWS Dan Farrell

september '69

Seaver vs. Jenkins: Batters Stay Loose

by Red Foley

*T*he duck season, which Bill Hands and Jerry Koosman began with undue suddenness in the series opener, threatened to continue when the slumping Cubs and the surging Mets concluded their two-game confrontation at soggy Shea last night.

Monday's match, like some others between these two clubs in recent years, contained an added dimension—dusters. Although it was conjectural, it was also expected that both sides would be seeking redress in the finale.

Thus, with Tom Seaver and Fergy Jenkins doing the firing, the game-and-a-half margin that separated the two clubs in the tightening Eastern Division race wasn't nearly as close as some of their pitches figured to be.

Both have what Casey Stengel elegantly terms "a very small baseball." It was expected that hitters on either side would stay unbelievably loose.

As a rule, neither Seaver nor Jenkins is burdened by problems with control. But the circumstances of Monday's meeting, in which Koosman and Tommie Agee got decked and Ron Santo was hit, were enough to dictate a departure in that respect.

Santo, drilled in the right forearm just above the wrist, expected to attend last night's festivities. The precautionary X-rays taken yesterday were negative. The injury, although painful, didn't figure to keep the classy 29-year-old Cub third baseman out of the lineup.

"He won't be 100% and I expect he'll have a bit of trouble throwing, but I think Ron will play," a Cub spokesman said.

"Our pitchers don't have to be told what to do in these situations," replied Gil Hodges following the 3-2 win that enabled his Mets to square themselves with Chicago in the loss column.

The attempt to intimidate began when Hands low-bridged Agee in the first inning. He later backed the leadoff man away from the plate on a subsequent serve before Tommie concluded his turn with a roller to third.

When Santo led off the visitors' second, Koosman, who normally works the veteran slugger low and away, promptly jammed him. Santo, leaning in as usual, tried to duck. He didn't succeed.

Santo refused to withdraw following first aid and continued play despite considerable discomfort. His arm was encased in ice after the game and he spent a fitful night at the Cubs' midtown hotel.

"If I were in the game I'd do just what this boy did," Hodges said when asked about Koosman's delivery to Santo. "Our pitchers know all about taking care of our people."

Hands tried to retaliate when Koosman came to bat in the third, Bud Harrelson, who'd singled, was aboard. When Kooz tried to advance him, he wound up pop-bunting the ball in self-defense. Squared to sacrifice, Koosman had all he could do to get his bat up before Hands' pitch nailed him between the eyes.

Intimidation is an old Leo Durocher tactic. He employed it when he managed the Dodgers and again

None of the Mets, including Tom Seaver pictured here, would dig in too deeply at the plate after all the beanballs that were flying in the first game of the series against the Cubs.

while directing the Giants. Now, with his Cubs in a five-game slide and their once-mighty 9 1/2-game bulge nearly melted, it appears the Little Leader is up to his old tricks.

But the Mets, for one, aren't going to be duped. Koosman's swift and unrelenting reply to Durocher's "stick it in his ear" diplomacy readily indicates these Mets can be challenged but not cowered.

Santo, always an aggressive player, won't show the white feather. It's not his style and brushbacks, knockdowns and dusters won't alter his game.

He didn't become the best third baseman in the league by adopting a defensive posture. Santo has been hit by Met pitchers before. His most serious accident being the fractured left cheekbone he suffered after being struck with a pitch thrown by Jack Fisher in 1966.

Santo required immediate surgery, but missed only seven games before returning to the lineup. He comes to play and that's what he does best. In nine seasons with the Cubs, Santo has missed only 15 games.

In one particular case, the brushback, which the late Branch Rickey used to call "the purpose pitch," helped the Mets neutralize one of Santo's former teammates. They employed it as a defensive weapon against Adolfo Phillips in 1967, a year in which the fleet Panamian was gleefully padding his home run and RBI totals at their expense.

Soon afterward that Met moundsman began to shave Phillips. He didn't like it and that's all the reaction they needed. That's one reason why the Mets, by relying on an occasional brushback, have been keeping Phillips honest ever since.

Maybe that tactic doesn't work with Santo, but the very fact the Mets have such a weapon does serve as a deterrent to other players.

Whether the National League should have replaced its umpires with game wardens remains to be seen. But if the Cubs did decide to reopen the duck season, they did so knowing the Mets were also ready to bag their limit. ■

Kooz Explains Why He Had to Deck Santo

by Dick Young

Okay," said Jerry Koosman. "Yes, I threw at him, but don't make it sound like I'm bragging about it, because I'm not."

He stood in front of the long mirror above the sinks in the Mets' john, combing his hair. He had been asked the same question maybe 20 times, maybe 120 times, and he had insisted it was just a coincidence that his pitch hit Ron Santo after the Cub pitcher had knocked down Tommie Agee. Now, the 121st time he was telling it like it is. This is modern baseball's small piece of old-fashioned jungle tradition.

"They threw at Tommie," said Jerry Koosman. "I had to do it to end it right there. If I don't, they keep doing it, and they keep getting away with it. I've seen it. I've seen three, four, five of our guys get knocked down and our pitcher never come close to their men."

To most professionals, it is the code of the hills. An eye for an eye, a head for a head, a knockdown for a knockdown.

"You don't have to talk about things like that," said Gil Hodges. He had been asked if there had been talk on the Mets' bench after Tommie Agee went down, talk of getting even. "Talk isn't necessary.

> "They threw at Tommie. I had to do it to end it right there. If I don't, they keep doing it, and they keep getting away with it."
>
> —Jerry Koosman

They know what to do for each other. Our boys will take care of our boys," said Hodges.

"Nobody said anything to me," confirmed Jerry Koosman. "I've got to do it, and I'll do it again. If Tommie doesn't think I'm working for him, he won't work for me—and I want Tommie Agee working for me. He and Cleon, they're the two best hitters I have out there. I want them both working for me."

It is commonly thought that a wave of indignant rage sweeps the bench when a teammate goes down, and that threats of vengeance are spat among the cuss words. Misconception. When Agee got back to the bench in the first frame, after eating dirt, he said nothing to Jerry Koosman and Koosman said nothing to him.

"If a guy's pitching, he's a pro. I don't have to go to him," said Tommie Agee. "He knows what's going on. Down the stretch, I'm gonna get thrown at more and more. Our pitchers can't let us get run off the field." ■

Wild! Mad! Beautiful! Mets .002 Out, 7-1

by Red Foley

Leo Durocher switched from Ken Holtzman to Ferguson Jenkins last night. By the time the Mets had run up a 7-1 lead after seven, the Cubs' skipper was probably wondering why he bothered.

Tom Seaver, looking for his 21st victory and the win that would narrow the Cubs' lead to a mere half game over the surging Mets, opposed Jenkins. The paid attendance was 51,448 but there was an overall 58,436 in the park.

Seaver disposed of the Cubs in order in the first inning, then took a 2-0 cushion to the mound in the next. Jenkin's wildness, plus a full-count meatball he served Boswell, produced the lead. ■

There had to be more than luck to the Mets' climb. But a black cat walking in front of the Cubs' dugout didn't harm the Mets.

National League Eastern Division
As of September 11

Team	Wins	Losses	Percentage	Games Back
METS	84	57	.596	—
Chicago	84	59	.587	1
St. Louis	77	65	.542	7 1/2
Pittsburgh	75	64	.540	8
Philadelphia	56	84	.400	27 1/2
Montreal	44	99	.308	41

september '69

We're No. 1!
We Really Are!

Mets Sweep into 1st, 3-2, 7-1

by Dana Mozley

At 8:43 last night, the Amazin' Mets, who in eight years have run the gamut from unintentional comedians to confident, gifted athletes, moved into first place in the National League's Eastern Division. At 11:38, after completing their twi-night sweep of the Expos, 3-2 and 7-1, they could sleep on a full one-game cushion over the Cubs.

In reaching heights never thought possible in the year 1969—Chicago led them by 9 1/2 games on August 13—the Mets pulled off their Little Miracle of Flushing with two out in the 12th inning of the Shea opener.

When Cleon Jones' single, Rod Gaspar's walk and Ken Boswell's single just out of the reach of second baseman Gary Sutherland added up to the winning run, two things quickly happened:

Club owner Mrs. Joan Shipman Payson was beckoned out of her first-row box and received the plaudits and thanks of the 23,512 fans as, dressed in royal purple, she walked to the exit behind home plate.

When Nolan Ryan completed his three-hit triumph—all of them within the infield—not long before midnight and the Bruins had been eaten up in Philadelphia, the scoreboard lines were brought up to date.

While the Mets may have appeared as relaxed and loose before their night of reckoning— "They're confident but not overconfident," promised manager Gil Hodges—the pressure got to them once the action began. They made errors, both actual and mental. They struck out 16 times in the first game and

would never have reached overtime if it hadn't been for a pitching balk.

Once they did get into extra innings, they just had to win. For the poor Expos, who are now leading San Diego as the losingest club in the majors, have been in 12 overtimes. Not only haven't they won any of them, but they have yet to even score after the ninth inning.

DAILY NEWS   John Duprey

High-Flying Mets Toast Their Newfound Status

by Larry Fox

A midst popping champagne corks, the Amazin' Mets last night held a mini-celebration as the clock struck 12. They had just turned from baseball's pumpkins into the first-place carriage trade. For the first time in their eight-year life, they were No. 1.

"How does it feel to be with a winner?" somebody said to Yogi Berra, who was part of 11 of 14 Yankee pennants.

Berra laughed. "Great!" he said.

"He's the last New York manager to win a pennant," said somebody, dredging up the fateful 1964 race.

"You gave all us Italians a bad name," said coach Joe Pignatano.

"How?" said Yogi.

"By blowing the World Series, dummy," said Piggy.

"I was gone anyhow," said Yogi, who was fired in one of baseball's strangest post-season developments.

The corks popped nearby, and Tom Seaver poured into paper cups for the boys.

Where did the bubbly come from, somebody wanted to know. Had Gil Hodges sprung?

"No," said Seaver. "Some of the guys visited a winery this afternoon and brought back three bottles of champagne, and three of sparkling burgundy."

They toasted Ken Boswell, whose bouncing hit had put them in first place by beating Montreal in the 12th inningof the first game. They toasted Nolan Ryan, who had fireballed the distance in the easy second win.

"I felt if I didn't do it somebody else would have," Boswell was telling newsmen. "But I'm glad it was me. I'll always remember it." ∎

Wham! Mets Win 10th on Ron's Slam, 5-2

September 14, 1969
by Dick Young

Rocky Swoboda, one of the most amazin of the Amazin' Mets, today powered the first grandslam of his colorful big-league life. The tremendous shot, clearing the left-center wall above the 406-foot sign, smashed a 1-1 tie with the Pirates and gave the Mets the ultimate 5-2 ball game, 10th straight win on a surge that has swept them into first place by three lengths, pending the outcome of tonight's Cub clash in St. Loo.

The blast also provided Tom Seaver with his 22d win. It came off Twiggy Hartenstein, who had just relieved lefty Luke Walker. Oddly, Swoboda looked awful against the southpaw. So had most of the other righty hitters in the lineup.

Hartenstein came in to face Donn Clendenon. Catcher Manny Sanguillen let a pitch get away. That moved the men to second and third and prompted an intentional pass to Clendenon.

Up came Swoboda. He looked at a ball, then swung at a fastie, up and away. That's how it went out, and when Rocky got home, upon completion of what he calls his addie Trot, the other three were waiting there to pat him on his invulnerable head.

Mets Unstrung, 5-3: Lead Still 3 1/2

by Dick Young

Again the pitcher for the Amazin' Mets banged an unexpected hit to drive in a big run today. But the Pirate pitcher did it, too, an even bigger run, and that was the story of the 5-3 defeat that ended the spectacular 10-game winning streak. The Cub defeat by St. Loo averted a loss of ground, however, so the Mets actually gained a day in the pursuit of their preposterous dream as their lead stayed at 3 1/2 games.

Nolan Ryan and Steve Blass were the pitchers involved. Nolan banged in the knotting run in the sixth, with Ed Charles on second and two down. Blass singled in the seventh with two on, two down, and the count 2-and-2, smashing the 3-3 tie.

There was a second-guess. Gil Hodges had ordered a walk for Fred Patek. He's Pitt's Tiny Tim, the 5-foot-4 shortstop. What is the second-guess about walking a No. 8 hitter to get at the pitcher with a man on second and two out? Only that Steve Blass is not the automatic out most pitchers are. He is batting .254. Patek is .246.

"They should have scouted me in Chicago," said Steve Blass, grinning. "That day, they walked Patek and I hit a home run." Blass got four hits that day. ∎

Ron's HRs Top Carlton's 19 K Mark

September 16, 1969
by Dick Young

The Mets were absolutely no match for Steve Carlton tonight, yet beat him, 4-3, which only goes to prove how utterly amazin they really are. They struck out 19 times, more times than anybody has in a nine-inning game in all of baseball history, but Ron Swoboda, the inconstant hero, made contact twice and drove the ball out of the park each time with a man on.

In such ludicrously fantastic fashion did the Mets boom 4 1/2 lengths ahead in their pursuit of the preposterous dream— 4 1/2 ahead of the collapsing Cubs with 15 to go, and if that isn't a lock it's at least a hinge.

"It's great to win when you play badly," said Gil Hodges, referring to the 19 whiffs and to the four errors his team made. They got away luckily with the flubs; none came in a scoring inning. Gary Gentry and Tug McGraw were able to fire out of the adversity, and Mac became the winning beneficiary of Swoboda's shot in the eighth.

NL East as of September 16

Team	Wins	Losses	Percentage	Games Back
METS	89	58	.605	—
Chicago	85	63	.574	4 1/2
St. Louis	79	68	.537	10
Pittsburgh	77	69	.527	11 1/2
Philadelphia	59	87	.404	29 1/2

1 9 6 9
September 19

Mets Fly Home 5 Up; Seaver Wins 23rd, 2-0

by Dick Young

ith Commissioner Bowie Kuhn here to spectate, not investigate, the 100-1 shot Amazin' Mets tonight continued to make a shambles of the NL race. Tom Seaver, winning his 23rd, knocked off the Expos, 2-0, with Ed Kranepool, today's blueplate special, providing the homer power that zoomed the Amazin's five lengths in front with 13 to go.

The mathematics of that make the Magic No. 8 for the elimination of the Cubs and just three for the defending champ Cards.

This concludes the most spectacular road trip in Mets history, short, but how sweet it was…six of seven, with four shutouts. The Mets have won 91, which just happens to be as many as they won in their first two seasons combined. Somehow, they seem more than twice as good as those clubs.

Asked for a pre-plane comment as the team packed for home, manager Gil Hodges said: "I am very happy about it. We still have to go out and win."

They went out and won two shutouts here in two nights, and now haven't allowed a run for 22 innings. The strong staff has clicked off 24 shutouts, six by Seaver. His 23 wins tie him with Denny McLain and Mike Cuellar for big-league leadership. He whiffed nine for a nice, round 200 on the year.

The Mets' incredible pullaway has been likened to the running of the classic horse-race, with the winner laying back till the eighth pole, September 10; while letting Chi set the pace all the way, then coming on and running away with each stride. Somebody mentioned it to Seaver after tonight's game. "The only thing," said Seaver, "is this race is being won by an eight-year-old maiden." ∎

National League Eastern Division
As of September 19

Team	Wins	Losses	Percentage	Games Back
METS	91	58	.611	—
Chicago	87	64	.576	5
St. Louis	80	69	.537	11
Pittsburgh	79	70	.530	12
Philadelphia	60	89	.403	31
Montreal	48	103	.318	44

Pirates Waylay Flagship, 8-2, 8-0

by Phil Pepe

When the Pirates got through with them last night, the Mets had nothing left but their lead over the Cubs. Gone was their mini-streak of three games, their shutout string that had reached 23 innings and their record of not allowing the opposition a home run that had gone through 23 games and 221 innings.

The Pirates slapped the Amazing Ones down twice, but hard, sweeping the doubleheader by scores of 8-2 and 8-0, with left-handers Bob Veale and Luke Walker getting complete games.

A crowd of 51,885 jammed Shea Stadium, hoping to watch the Mets inch closer to their first title and ready to cheer them when they did. As it turned out, the only real cheering the fans were able to do was for the Cardinals, who knocked off the second-place Cubs in the second game of their doubleheader. In that respect, the night wasn't a total loss. The Mets' double dip coupled with the Cubs split shaved a game off New York's lead, now four games, five in the losing column. It also dropped the magic number for a Met clinching to seven.

Outside of that, there was little to cheer about as the Mets dropped a double header for the first time since the Astros beat them here on July 30. ∎

Poor Leo, or It Couldn't Happen to a Nicer Guy

September 17, 1969
by Dick Young

"Poor Leo." Wherever I go these days, in dugouts, clubhouses, in the offices of general managers, I hear the same words. Everybody is so sorry for Leo Durocher over the way the Cubs have fallen apart. The only thing I wonder about is that everybody is smiling like crazy when they say it.

"Poor Leo," said Joe Brown, who general manages the Pitts. His team had just put a deep dent in the Cubs' pennant plans. The Pitts had played some of their best ball against Chicago.

"Don't you think everybody is trying just a little bit harder to beat the Cubs?" said Joe Brown. "They all seem to want to beat Durocher."

I wondered about that. Does it really work that way at this time of year? Do ballplayers who are not directly involved in the pennant chase take a particular delight in knocking off a team whose manager has devoted his life to making people hate him?

1 9 6 9
September 21

Moose 0-Hitter Mortifies Mets, 4-0

Don't Panic! Magic No. Cut to 6

by Phil Pepe

There were 58,893 fans at Shea yesterday and they went home happy. They had seen a no-hitter. But it wasn't a Met who piched the no-hitter, it was Bob Moose, who held the Amazing Ones hitless as the Pirates waltzed to a 4-0 victory.

Still the fans were happy. The Cubs lost to the Cardinals and the Mets held their lead at four games, five on the losing side and reduced their magic number to six. Only the Mets can fail to get a hit and still send their fans home happy.

In sending the Mets down to their third straight defeat, Moose, a hard-throwing curveballing right-hander, struck out six and faced only three men over the minimum 27. The only Mets base runners were Ron Swoboda, who walked with one out in the second; Ed Kranepool, who walked with one out in the fifth; and Rod Gaspar, who walked as a pinch-hitter for reliever Tug McGraw leading off the ninth.

The closest thing to a hit came with two out in the sixth, when Wayne Garrett drove one to deep right. "I thought it was gone when he hit it," Moose said, "but then I saw the wind hold it up. I knew if any rightfielder was going to catch it, Clemente would."

Roberto went back to the fence, leaped and caught the ball one-handed to preserve the no-hitter. After that there wasn't anything resembling a hit. ■

Metsomania — By Bill Gallo

AND IN THE TOP OF THE SIXTH, THE METS LEAD PITTSBURGH...

HELLO, ALEX!

september '69

Mets Sweep, 5-3, 6-1; Magic No. 4

by Phil Pepe

Jerry Koosman reminded the Mets how to win in the first game and Don Cardwell took the cue in the second as the Mets swept the Pirates in a double-header, 5-3 and 6-1, at Shea Stadium yesterday to reduce their magic number to four.

A crowd of 55,991, largest in the NL this year, saw Koosman break a three-game Met losing streak to win his 16th in the opener, then stayed to watch Cardwell hang up his fifth game since May 6 in the nightcap.

Veteran right-hander Don Cardwell tried to knock the number down a notch as he opposed Steve Blass in the second game.

Last year, 15 of Koosman's victories came after Met defeats, but none of them were as big as yesterday. Another defeat to the Pirates and panic might have started setting in. Kooz took good care of that in winning his 16th, what he called "a morale booster."

Koosman wasn't his usual overpowering self, only good enough to win. He struck out seven and put down the Bucs every time they threatened to break the game apart. He got tougher when the Mets gave him a cushion. In the eighth inning the crowds told him what was going on with the Cubs.

As the eighth inning started, a huge roar went up from the crowd. Koosman didn't even have to look around at the scoreboard.

"I knew what happened," he said, "I just didn't know how many."

What happened was the Cards took a temporary 2-1 lead over the Cubs in Chicago. And Koosman reacted to the roar by fanning Dave Cash and Willie Stargell to start the eighth. By then, Koosman had his 5-3 lead and there was no way he was going to give it up. ∎

DAILY NEWS

Tommie Agee trots home to score as Art Shamsky awaits his turn to bat.

september '69

1 9 6 9
September 22

Magic No. 3 on Tom's (24) Magic, 3-1

by Red Foley

 **T**om Seaver's 24th victory of the season and ninth in succession—this one a 3-1 Shea triumph over the Cardinals—dropped the Mets' magic number to three last night. A crowd of 23,627 saw the big righthander yield four hits as he became the winningest pitcher in the major leagues.

Nelson Briles, in suffering his 13th setback, was banged for all seven hits the Mets collected as they won their third in a row.

Seaver and Briles matched zips for three. Neither was perfect, but each was plenty good. Flood, legging a one-out hopper behind second in the opening inning, was St. Loo's lone baserunner over that span.

Grote produced the Mets' only hit—a two-out single to center after Briles had clipped Swoboda with a pitch in the second inning. Grote's single advanced Swoboda to third, but Briles, jamming Harrelson, induced the shortstop to pop harmlessly to Pinson for the final out.

Both pitchers were very sharp, but not in a strikeout sense. Their stuff was overpowering, but only Shannon, looking in the second, and Agee, gazing in the third, were victimized over the K route. ∎

Met Players Pick Their MVP—Guess Who?

September 24, 1969
by Dick Young

Who is MVP in the National League? If you had a vote, would it be Seaver? Would it be Agee? Or Cleon Jones? Maybe Pete Rose, you Yankee fan, you.

I asked the Mets players to vote. I told them to vote only for a Met. It's safer that way. You never know when there's a Billy Loes in the crowd and I didn't want a vote to show up with Ernie Banks' name on it, and be responsible for blood flowing in the Shea clubhouse.

The results of the player poll were interesting. Not too surprising, perhaps, but interesting:

Tom Seaver	14
Tommie Agee	9
Cleon Jones	3
Al Weis	1

That Al Weis vote intrigues me, inasmuch as each player was instructed not to vote for himself. Besides, Al Weis is the last guy in the world who would vote for himself. If you asked Al Weis to name the nicest man he knows with the initials A.W., he'd say Adolph Webelkampf.

september '69

Magic Number

2

Any combination of Mets wins and Cub losses clinches division title for Mets

Mets' No. Sliced to 2; Who Becomes No. 3?

by Phil Pepe

Ever cautious, ever cagey Gil Hodges says he has not thought about the National League playoff and will not begin thinking about the National League playoff until the Mets, in fact, are in it.

But Gil Hodges is always prepared. And it is because he is very cautious, ever cagey and ever ready, that Gil Hodges must have allowed himself some small thought about the playoff.

With the Mets' magic number a minuscule two following the Cubs' defeat by the Expos yesterday, and with a chance to knock it down to one with a victory over the Cardinals last night, the manager and his pitching coach Rube Walker have to begin thinking ahead. They have to start setting up their pitching for the playoff.

It doesn't take much of a genius to figure out that Hodges will open with Tom Seaver and follow with Jerry Koosman, and that Seaver and Kooz will come back if they are needed for games four and five. That leaves game No. 3 up for grabs.

The assignment is up for grabs among Gary Gentry, Don Cardwell, Nolan Ryan and Jim McAndrew, who went after his seventh victory against the Cardinals last night. He was opposed by Bob Gibson. McAndrew was motivated to impress the boss that he should get the playoff shot. ∎

National League Eastern Division

As of September 24

Team	Wins	Losses	Percentage	Games Back
METS	94	61	.606	—
Chicago	89	67	.571	5 1/2
St. Louis	82	72	.532	11 1/2
Pittsburgh	82	72	.532	11 1/2
Philadelphia	61	92	.399	32
Montreal	52	104	.333	42 1/2

september '69

1 9 6 9
September 24

Mets Down Gibson, Champagne Today?

by Phil Pepe

Bud Harrelson lined a single to left with one out in the 11th, as the Mets beat Bob Gibson and the Cardinals, 3-2, to reduce their magic number to one as 32,364 happy fans looked on at Shea last night.

Harrelson's single followed infield hits by Ron Swoboda and Jerry Grote with one out and assured the Mets of no worse than a tie for the NL East title with six games remaining. The Mets can clinch their division before they go to the ballpark tonight. A Cub defeat to the Expos in the afternoon does it. If the Cubs win, the Mets can wrap it up by beating the Cardinals at night.

Jim McAndrew (6-7) opposed Bob Gibson, the Tom Seaver of 1968, who was trying to win his 19th.

Gibson needed two victories in three starts, including last night, to become a 20-game winner for the fourth time in the last five years. The only time he missed was in 1967, when he was out eight weeks with a broken foot.

The Mets broke into the lead, scoring a run off Gibson in the third, when Harrelson led with a walk, moved to second as Agee rolled out and scored on Garrett's seeing-eye bouncing single between the first-second hole.

Against McAndrew, the Cards were suffering from the same malady that plagued the 1968 NL Champs all season—lack of the big hit. They wasted Pinson's two-out double in the first, opening singles by Maxvill and Gibson in the third and Torre's leadoff single in the fourth. In each case, they let McAndrew off the hook, although Mac earned it. ∎

Met Fans Cheer Cubs—for a Day

September 25, 1969
by Pete Coutros

On any other day, it would have smacked of treachery but yesterday, somehow, it seemed to be perfectly defensible. There were Mets fans rooting for the Cubs and no one was looking to string them up on a lamp post.

The Cubs were playing Montreal in Chicago. If they lost, the Mets would be the National League's Eastern champs. But that would be backing in, as they say in baseball circles, and that kind of melts the icing on the cake.

So all the loyal citizens of Metsiana were rooting for the Cubs to win so the Mets could cop the divisional crown on their own, by beating the Cards at Shea last night.

W.S. Vet Berra Predicts Mets Can Take All with Hurlers

by Dana Mozley

As it takes one who knows one, it is of considerable interest—and importance—that Lawrence Peter (Yogi) Berra feels these Miraculous Mets can well be the next champions of all baseball.

In a total of 15 World Series, all but one of them as a player, the Mets' first base coach has played on a record 10 winners.

"This is an amazin' team," said Yogi yesterday. Casey Stengel, Dick Young and many other people have come to the same conclusion at one point or another during the last eight years.

"If we hadn't won it this year, it would have been next year or the year after," the 44-year-old Berra decided. "They have championship written all over them."

"No one else in baseball is as well set up for a short series as we are. How would you like to meet Seaver and Koosman every fourth day? Ryan and Gentry and McAndrew and Cardwell can do the job, too. And our bullpen is about as good as you can find.

"This team is really amazin' the

way it stays loose. It's a young team but no one panics. And everyone pitches in. It seems there's a new hero every day.

"I haven't been in a World Series since 1964, but I'm sure I'll be in one this time. And what a great thrill that's going to be!" ■

DAILY NEWS

Mets coach Yogi Berra obliges a 12-year-old Met fan by autographing a copy of the color photo which appeared on page one of The News.

september '69

Millennium Is Here . . . Mets Champs

by Phil Pepe

*he Mets are champs. Say it again, it sounds so good. The Mets are champs. One more time because it's all so unbelievable. The Mets are champs.*

At precisely 9:06 p.m. last night, the Mets stopped being a joke. At precisely 9:06 last night, the Mets stopped being the symbol of frustration, ineptness and futility; stopped being the subject of ridicule.

At precisely 9:06, the Mets completed a short-second-first DP completing a 6-0 victory over the Cardinals, clinching the NL East title and touching off a celebration heard around the world. Confetti streamed down the field, firecrackers were set off and, within moments, fans swarmed on the field like locusts and Met players were trapped in a mass of jubilant humanity.

They chanted "we're No. 1" and, in their joy they clutched at everything in sight, Mets' caps, bases, even dirt from the pitcher's mound as they released the emotion that has been pent up since the Mets were officially formed seven years, seven months and seven days ago.

Hours after the final putout, they were still swarming over the field, refusing to go home, hoping to savor this moment of moments and trying to wash away the failures and the frustrations of the past eight seasons. They clustered around the Met dugout, imploring their heroes to come out. They cheered for Tom Seaver and Jerry Koosman and Tommie Agee and Cleon Jones and Donn Clendenon. But their heroes were inside their clubhouse, having a wild celebration of their own.

To a man, this is the way the Mets wanted to win it—in Shea in their last home game of the year, before a near-capacity crowd of 54,928 of their loyal fans and millions more watching on television and listening on radio.

To a man, the Mets didn't want to "back" into it—and they didn't have to. They could have been champs if the Cubs had lost in the afternoon, but the Cubs obliged—as they have for the last six weeks—by beating the Expos and permitting the Mets to win it all by themselves.

They embellished it with a four-hit shutout by rookie Gary Gentry, given the distinct honor of making baseball history.

Bud Harrelson got it started with a single to right and Tommie Agee walked. After Cleon Jones fanned, Donn Clendenon, who became a Met on June 15, bombed a tremendous home run over the center field fence. It was his 14th homer of the year, his 10th since becoming a Met and his 32d, 33d and 34th RBI as a Met, all of them big ones.

The Mets were not finished exploding. Ron Swoboda walked and Ed Charles, the oldest Met, bombed his third homer over the right-center fence. As Ed rounded third, he clapped his hands "to let the fans know this was it and because, at my age, I might not have any more left."

The Mets had a 5-0 lead and then it was 6-0 in the fifth on Clendenon's second homer of the game. The fans knew that was enough and they seemed hardly able to wait until the game was over and they could set off an explosion of their own. ∎

september '69

Mets fans swarm the field at Shea Stadium after the Mets clinched the first NL East title with a 6-0 win over the Cardinals.

National League Eastern Division

As of September 25

Team	Wins	Losses	Pct.	G.B.
METS	94	61	.606	—
Chicago	89	67	.571	5 1/2
St. Louis	82	72	.532	11 1/2
Pittsburgh	82	72	.532	11 1/2
Philadelphia	61	92	.399	32
Montreal	52	104	.333	42 1/2

Sheer Madness:
Champagne, Laughs, Arrests

by Dick Young

In the wildest victory celebration ever, surpassing Ebbets Field in 1955, the Amazin' Met players flooded their roaring clubhouse in champagne, while outside, the berserk fans were taking home Shea Stadium for a souvenir.

It wasn't till an hour after the end of the game, the clincher of the NL's pennant east, that dozens of specials and cops from the 109th Precinct herded thousands of lingering fans through an opening of the center field fence. They just wouldn't go home.

Several arrests were made, and two men were seen taken from the field handcuffed. The charge, undoubtedly, will be destruction of public property.

The outfield of Shea Stadium looks like the surface of the moon. Vari-sized craters have been created by the vulturous fans who swooped onto the field by the thousands and tore up clumps of grass to take home as memorabilia of this historic event. Six fractures were reported in the first aid room by Ruth Harden, RN, including three broken legs.

They clawed at the turf till craters six feet in diameter appeared. They made off with home plate and second base.

"We'll have it back in shape for the playoffs," said Jim Thomson, Met veep in charge of Shea. "Fortunately, the club is going on the road and we have more than a week. It's a mess. A wonderful mess."

In the clubhouse, the players were less violent, but equally uninhibited. Most of them obviously too young to appreciate champagne, they shook up the bottles and squirted it at each other. Nobody was spared.

Gil Hodges got the douse treatment from Tom Seaver, who screamed, "Congratulations, skip!"

Nolan Ryan, the bravest in all the land, poured bubbly over the head of Don Grant, chairman of the board.

Jerry Koosman showered his champagne bottle over nearby newsmen, and Ed Kranepool lifted his high and shouted, "Here's to Leo!"

The right side of Kranepool's face was puffed twice normal size. He'd had dental surgery the day before. Somebody told him to watch his jaw. "Screw the jaw!" said Krane, who had come here as a 17-year-old high school kid in '62, and suffered through more than the rest. "I waited too long for this!"

"I'm real happy," said Art Shamsky. "I hope my folks are proud of me now." Sham's parents wanted him to stay in school.

Lou Niss, traveling sec and an original Met, pointed to Dr. Peter LaMotte, Met physician. "Remember when Casey said Dr. LaMotte was the most valuable player on the club?" said Niss.

"Here's to Casey," roared some of the older Mets, bottles high. ∎

What Happened?
Decked Cards Try to Explain

by Dick Young

N ow that you have learned the thousand and one reasons why the Mets won it, all of them utterly amazin', one question needs be answered. Why did the Cardinals lose it?

What happened to this St. Louis team, this super team, which ran off and hid the year before? They had beaten nine other teams easily. Now, under the new divisional play, they would have to beat only five.

Cinch. Everybody knew it. Las Vegas knew it, and who knows better than Las Vegas? The day the race began, the official betting line came out of the West. The odds were issued for the pennant, not for divisional titles.

For example, behind the favored Cardinals came the Reds' at 7-2; then the Giants at 4-1, and the Braves at 6-1. The Cardinals, in other words, were such stickouts to take their division, three teams in the West were listed before you came to Chicago, considered the closest thing to competition that St. Louis would have in 1969.

The prices quoted on teams in the NL East were:

Cardinals	9-5
Cubs	8-1
Pirates	10-1
Phils	15-1
Mets	100-1
Expos	300-1

If the whole thing were to start right now, knowing what you know now and believing what

you have just seen, wouldn't the Cardinals be favored over the Mets? How does a 9-5 shot get beat by a 100-1 shot? Where did it go wrong, Red Schoendienst?

"Opening day," said the Cardinal manager. He laughed. "That's right," he said. "That's where it started. Pittsburgh beat us in 14 innings the first day, then we lost three straight, and we never got straightened around. We spent all season trying to get that man in from third base. We actually hit more than we did last year, but not at the right time." ■

Gil's Worry: Keepin' Pitchers Sharp
September 26, 1969
by Red Foley

Gil Hodges, no different from the rest of his merry Mets, woke up with a headache yesterday. But it was pitchers and not bottl that caused his cranial cloud. In fact, the boys at Excedrin don even have to bother coming up with a number for this one.

Keeping his pitchers sharp for the playoffs is Hodges' bigges problem. Actually, it began before the champagne shower and shaving cream shampoos were dispensed following Wednesday night's clinch.

Hodges has five no-count games and 10 do-count days in which to get Tom Seaver, Jerry Koosman and the rest of his moundsmen ready. Pitching put the Mets into the playoffs and it's the pitching that will have to transport them past the Wester Division survivor if a World Series is to follow.

Mets Give Hodges Pact Fit for Kingpin

by Dick Young

" *He gets a three-year contract," said Bud Harrelson, "and we get a weekend in Philadelphia."*

DAILY NEWS   Paul DeMaria

It had just been revealed, in a hurriedly called press conference at Shea Stadium, that Gil Hodges' contract has been torn up and a new one agreed to. The old one had a year to run. The new one, like his first, calls for three years, through 1972.

The Met players are happy for Gil. For themselves, too. Especially for themselves. The gratuitous action by the people who write the checks for the Mets signals a generous spirit, and they'll get theirs next. "If I'm not traded," said Ed Kranepool, the most mind-traded man on the club.

"I hope there's some left for us," said Bud Harrelson with that little-boy grin of his.

A good guess at the manager's new salary is $70,000. That's a $10,000 raise. What's more, it's retroactive for the 1969 season, instant reward for riding the Mets on top of the NL East. This amounts to a 10-grand bonus.

Mets manager Gil Hodges (left) and GM Johnny Murphy beam after announcing that Hodges' contract has been extended three more years.

Add to that the $25,000 full share he stands to pull down if the Amazins win the World Series, and toss in his good health, and this has been a rewarding year for Gil Hodges. A year ago he was flat on his back in an Atlanta hospital, not knowing if his heart would let him manage again. ∎

Cleon Drives for Bat Title at Leadoff

by Dick Young

Having taken care of the number one item, finishing first, Gil Hodges today opened his drive on the NL batting title—for Cleon Jones. Hodges elevated Jones from third in the batting order to leadoff in hopes of getting Cleon to bat an extra time in the ballgame. An extra time; perhaps an extra hit.

"I wish I had done it last night," said Hodges, just before Jones went up swinging against Philly's Grant Jackson. "He might have got up an extra time and avoided the collar. I felt bad when Kranepool got thrown out."

The Mets fell two men short of bringing Cleon up in the ninth. Prior to that, he had gone 3-for-0 dipping two points to .341. The leader, Pete Rose, picked up three more hits and boomed to .347.

It is tough to pickup six points with four games to go, especially on Rose. Last year, Charley Hustle overtook Pitty's Matty Alou in the last days.

Hodges' reference to Kranepool getting thrown out happened in last night's seventh inning. Ed had singled with two down. A pitch got past the catcher and rolled perhaps 20 feet to the rear. Krane hesitated, then took off and was nailed.

This, plus a DP grounder next inning by Duffy Dyer, were late-game developments that deprived Jones of his chance to get up in the ninth.

"When I got to the park today," said Hodges, "I talked the idea over with Cleon, and he said he liked the idea of batting first."

"It not only gets me up a few more times for the rest of the season," Cleon said, "but I'll get better pitches to hit." ■

Mets Net 4th Zip in Row

September 29, 1969
by Dick Young

The best young pitching staff in baseball, which already has won the NL East for the Mets, today set a club high for consecutive scoreless innings while beating the Phils, 2-0.

The combined shutout was worked by three pitchers and pushed the Mets' amazin' victory total to 99. They have won eight straight, and need only split the two remaining games in Chicago to reach 100, their new magic number.

And there is a very special sentimental reason for wanting to do this. The Avengers would consider it an eradication of the 100-defeat season endured by the original Mets of 1962.

This was the Mets' fourth straight shutout, also unprecedented in their annals. The perpetrators have been Gary Gentry then Jerry Koosman, Tom Seaver and Gentry, with Nolan Ryan and Ron Taylor sharing the fourth.

Mets Make the Most of Lively Ol' Ball, 7-6

by Red Foley

A lively crowd and an even livelier baseball was on display when the Mets edged the Yankees, 7-6, in their annual Mayor's Trophy match last night at Shea. The crowd, which numbered 32,720, lasted longer than the baseballs, which numbered five dozen.

As a test, the umpires opened the game by using the new experimental baseball, which the manufacturers claim has 10% more hop than the normal ball now in use. The insertion of the "lively" ball was not made known to the players. But once plate umpire Paul Pryor ran out of the rabbits they had to realize the difference.

Pryor's supply was exhausted after five innings, by which time the clubs had scored a dozen runs and banged 16 of the total 22 hits they collected. Beginning with the sixth inning, when Pryor switched from baseballs autographed by "Bugs Bunny" to the customary National League balls signed by Warren Giles, the game began to acquire a touch of normalcy.

It retained it only until Steve Hamilton took over the Yankee pitching in the sixth. The angular lefty animated both the fans and the Mets the rest of the way by throwing his famed "folly floater."

That's the poor man's "eephus" pitch, the one on which he hesitates at the top of his delivery and then pushes the ball in an arc that probably reaches

DAILY NEWS

Yankees manager Ralph Houk and Mets manager Gil Hodges shake hands before the Mayor's Trophy Game.

20 feet before starting its downward glide.

Tommie Agee and Rod Gaspar both swung against it in the Mets' eighth. They both hit it, but didn't drive the pitch past the infield. By then the Mets were leading 7-5, with all but two of their runs being driven in by Art Shamsky. ∎

september '69

Mets Down Cubs, 6-5, in 12 for 100th Win

by Dick Young

There was meaning in today's 6-5 Met win over the Cubs, their ninth straight, beyond the meaning of Gil Hodges and Leo Durocher master-minding it like crazy for 12 innings with lefty-righty switches into the dusk.

The game wound up with pinch-hitter Art Shamsky banging a left-handed single off reliever Hank Aguirre's only left-handed pitch, and that was win No. 100 for the Avengers.

A month or so ago, the meaning of these games, today and tomorrow, was to be immense, or so most folks believed. 'Twas thought the entire NL East pennant would boil down to these games, and that is why there were 10,136 roaring fans here today. They had bought their tickets a month ago, they and many more who took the loss and stayed away.

The Mets, champs now for a week, played this one to the hilt because they were going for win No. 100, and there's something special about wanting to win 100 when you have been known to lose more than 100 most of your life.

The Cubs, too, were all out. They had blown a 9 1/2-game lead to the Mets, and this game, if they

The New York Mets work on cutting an album. Shown here are (l to r) Art Shamsky, Ken Boswell and Tug McGraw.

could win it, would wipe away a small piece of the shame; wipe it away, at least, for the 10,000 faithful who were in the stands screaming their heads off, and getting in a fight here and there with some member of the Met minority, foolhardy enough to wear a blue cap with NY on the crown. ∎

Mets Drop 5-3 Kiss-off to Cubs

October 3, 1969
by Dick Young

Twenty years from today, when Bob Holreiser is looking around for some fitting subject for his nostalgic cartoon "This Day in Sports," he might try: "The Amazin Mets concluded their amazin season with 100 victories by losing to the Cubs, 5-3, and then went on to Atlanta for the NL playoffs.

Or: "Cleon Jones went 2-for-5 to fail in his bid for the NL title. After leading the league for most of the season, Cleon finished with .340, third behind Pete Rose and Roberto Clemente."

Or: "Gary Gentry escaped serious injury when a line drive ricocheted off his wrist and struck him on the pitching shoulder."

Or: (For the Chicago clientele): "Ernie Banks, age 38, a triple, to keep Amazin Mets from winning 101."

National League Eastern Division
Final Standings

Team	Wins	Losses	Pct.	G.B.
METS	100	62	.617	—
Chicago	92	70	.568	8
St. Louis	88	74	.543	12
Pittsburgh	87	75	.537	13
Philadelphia	63	99	.389	37
Montreal	52	110	.321	48

september '69

DAILY NEWS

Bud Harrelson

Harrelson at SS:
A 12-Month Effort

by Dick Young

The sharp ground ball skipped predictably toward the Mets' shortstop. Bud Harrelson scooped it and fired to second base, where the second baseman pivoted and threw to first. It was the classic phantom double play. Atlanta did not have a runner on first base at the time.

"It was the most embarrassing moment of my life," said Bud Harrelson afterward.

Fortunately for Bud Harrelson, it did not mean the ball game. The Mets worked out of the mess his mental blank had created. There had been a man on second at the time, not first. Had it been most anyone but Felipe Alou, the man would have been out, even on two throws, and the side retired. Instead, Gary Gentry, perhaps cursing his fate, walked the next man. That brought up Hank Aaron, who is no man to bring up with bases full.

Hank Aaron had hit two homers this season off rookie Gary Gentry. This time Aaron picked his pitch, and drove it, humming, to leftfield. Rod Gaspar scurried back to the fence and turned. The ball began to sink. He reached up and grabbed it, and Bud Harrelson said a small "thank-you-God" as he trotted off the field.

"If that ball had gone out," said Bud Harrelson, "I'd have gone into that tepee and stayed there." The Braves have erected a tepee beyond the leftfield fence, where resides their cheerleading chief, Soc-A-Homa. Added Harrelson: "They'd have had to trade me to Atlanta to get me out."

"Just one of those things," said Gil Hodges. As a rule Gil Hodges does not dismiss mental lapses so lightly. But Bud Harrelson has played such great shortstop this year, Hodges felt he had a booboo coming. ("Great shortstop" are Hodges' words.)

"He goes back for a pop fly as good as anyone I've ever seen," said Gil Hodges, who grew up with Pee Wee Reese, pop-fly master of another time.

For a further rundown on Harrelson, the manager said: "He has good range at shortstop, good hands, good arm, and an attitude that is A-1."

He also has a rather small batting average. "He should improve as a hitter," says Gil Hodges. "He should be bunting more for base hits. Of course, they play him tough.

Hodges thinks that if Bud Harrelson can hit .250 he'll have a rewarding career in the majors. In 1967, Bud Harrelson hit .254. He hasn't been close since. Last year he played virtually one-legged. A knee cartilage was torn, and during the winter, the club surgeon, Dr. Peter LaMotte, removed it.

"I can run as good as ever now," said Bud Harrelson, the Mini-Hawk. That's what his teammates call him, Mini-Hawk. It derives from the other Harrelson, Ken, known as The Hawk. Bud Harrelson's beak is somewhat smaller than the Hawk's. So is the rest of him. Bud is 5-foot-11, 155 pounds when he's eating well, and looks bonier than that. He has been lifting weights during the off-seasons. He lifts them in a curling motion, in front of him, to develop his wrists and forearms and still not knot up his chest and shoulders.

"Hitting," said Bud Harrelson, "is from the elbows down."

Tips on Covering Second Base

When there's a man on first, the shortstop and second baseman must predetermine who will cover if the runner goes. I call it for our team. I hold up my glove in front of my mouth. I don't shout anything. I just hold my mouth open or closed for him to see. Open means I'll cover; closed, he'll cover.

—Bud Harrelson

Met fan Karl Ehrhardt makes sure the Mets gave their all. There was little doubt about the Mets' effort as they swept the Braves in three games.

N ot bad for underdogs.

Facing 8-to-5 favorites and the heavy hitters of the Atlanta Braves, the Mets more than held their own. In fact, the Mets overpowered the Braves with a five-run eighth inning to win the series opener, 9-5, in Atlanta.

The Mets jumped on the Braves hard in the second game with an eight-run lead in the fourth inning and held on for an 11-6 win—just a game away from a sweep.

And that's what they did. With home runs by Ken Boswell, Tommie Agee and Wayne Garrett, and a total of 14 hits, the Mets swept the Braves in three straight games. It also took Nolan Ryan's seven innings of solid relief pitching to complete the sweep after starter Gary Gentry was shelled in the first two innings. The Amazins scored 27 runs on 37 hits in the series, dismantling one of the hardest-hitting lineups in the National League, featuring Hank Aaron, Orlando Cepeda and Rico Carty.

With the Braves now behind them, the World Series loomed just ahead for the Mets. And as long as the field at Shea Stadium could be fixed in time after another round of boisterous celebration, the Mets were scheduled to host the Orioles after a pair of games in Baltimore.

Playoff Matchups: Mets Pick in NL

by Phil Pepe

*irst Base*—*Combined, the offensive figures of Clendenon and Kranepool match those of Cepeda. It's unlikely that either Met would match Cha Cha at bat, if he played full-time. Cepeda has a history of failure in World Series games, but his strength and power make him a home-run threat anytime he's swinging and Cha Cha takes his swings.* **Edge: Braves**

Second Base—Boswell is no match for Millan on defense, and anybody else the Mets put on second would be no match for Felix with the bat.

Edge: Braves.

Shortstop—Harrelson's defensive work has gained the respect of the Braves. They consider him as good as any shortstop in the league, the guts of the Met defense. Garrido came fast, but is not Bud's equal in the field or at bat.

Edge: Mets.

Third Base—There is still none better with the glove than Boyer, he of the lightning reflexes and the shotgun arm. Neither Garrett, Pfeil nor Charles can compare with Clete at bat or in the field.

Edge: Braves.

Left field—Closest matchup. Offensively, it's a standoff on average, but Carty has an edge over Jones on power. Cleon gets higher grades on speed, base running, throwing and fielding. Either Jones or Carty could get hot at bat and carry his club into the World Series.

Edge: Mets.

Center field—Agee's speed, power, defense and record of coming up with the big play all year make him the Mets' key man outside of pitchers. Gonzalez has hit well in the stretch and gets on base for Aaron, Carty and Cepeda. But Agee has it over Tony in all departments and, with Harrelson and Grote, gives the Mets strength where the Braves are weak—up the middle.

Edge: Mets.

Right field—No contest. Aaron is an all-timer who should be compared with DiMaggio and Mays, not Shamsky and Swoboda. He can win three games with his bat. At 35, he's dangerous as ever and shows no sign of slowing up in the outfield or on the bases. Shamsky and Swoboda have home run power, but pity Art and Ron because they are in the wrong positions for comparison and are overmatched by a great one.

Edge: Braves.

Catching—Defensively, Grote gets the nod over rookie Didier on his arm and experience.

Edge: Mets.

Pitching—The Mets' strong suit. Not only Seaver and Koosman, but in depth, Reed, winner of 11 of his last 14, may give the Mets more trouble than Niekro. For games three and four, Jarvis and Stone don't make it with Gentry and Cardwell…or McAndrew and Ryan for that matter.

Edge: Mets.

Bullpen—Without Wilhelm, the Braves wouldn't have won the NL West and they'll be without him for the playoffs.

Bench—Mets will platoon more, going to Weiss and Pfeil for defense, Swoboda, Garrett or Boswell for offense. ■

Mets manager Gil Hodges signals to his players on the field during the inaugural National League Championship Series.

Houk Sees O's Mets' Finale

by Joe Trimble
October 2, 1969

As a member of the Loyal Opposition, Ralph Houk's head and heart are not in accord. The Yankee manager, speaking as a professional believes the Orioles will go all the way but he adds the heartfelt opinion that the Mets could do it "with those two pitchers."

Ralphie didn't go so far as to pin one on Bill Gallo's "Go, Mets" buttons to his pinstripes but he wished Gil and his giddy kiddies all the best.

Mets Glad It's Braves

by Dick Young
October 3 , 1969

The Mets are glad to be here. A year ago, the Mets would have been glad to be anywhere, but now they are winners and can afford to be picky, and most of them have picked Atlanta as the team I-would-most-like-to-play-for-the-pennant.

From time to time, while San Francisco, Atlanta, and the Reds were playing musical chairs with first place in the Wild Wild West, I went around asking the Mets which team they would prefer to take on, and why.

Most said the Braves. A few said the Giants. None said the Reds, if that makes Dave Bristol feel any better. And when Houston was mentioned, back when that was a possibility, there were gasps, like I had said a dirty word. The Mets' 2-and-10 season record against the Astros explains that.

Majors' First Playoffs Open Today

Mets Are Underdogs

by Phil Pepe

ot one impossible dream come true, not one set of games played with the pomp and ceremony, the pressure and excitement of a World Series, but two. Not one super pitcher, but two.

That was the bargain offered to 50,000 fans in Atlanta Stadium and millions more watching on national television as the National League roared into the climax of its 101st year with its first inter-division playoff championship. And a more unlikely pairing would be hard to find. If you had bet in April that the Mets and Braves would be meeting in the best-of-five playoff series to determine the National League champion, they would have rushed you off to the looney bin. But you would be the richest man in the place. The Mets were rated 100-1 to win the NL East. The Braves were considered twice as good at 50-1 to give the NL West a Southern representative.

It's a series that has the basic elements of a classic baseball confrontation—good hitting against good pitching. But the Braves insist they have good pitching, too, and for tomorrow the key men are Niekro (23-13) and Seaver (25-7), the league's two biggest winners.

The 13-10 odds on the series favoring the Braves and 11-10 (6-5 man-to-man) in the first game are surprising because the Mets won eight of 12 from the Braves in the regular season and Seaver was 3-0 against the Braves. Niekro was 0-3 against the Mets. ∎

Hodges went with what he called "my left-handed hitting lineup," as follows:

Tommie Agee, CF

Wayne Garrett, 3B

Cleon Jones, LF

Art Shamsky, RF

Ken Boswell, 2B

Ed Kranepool, 1B

Jerry Grote, C

Bud Harrelson, SS

Tom Seaver, P

What Odds?

October 4, 1969
by Gil Hodges

I see where the Braves are the favorites over the Mets, and rightfully so, but it really doesn't mean a thing. These boys have been underdogs all year. They've been underdogs since 1962.

When you consider they've knocked down the odds from 100-1 to 13-10, I'd say my players have done a pretty good job. No matter what the odds are, if your pitching is right, and we play the kind of defensive ball we can, we should win it.

I wrestled with one lineup problem till this morning. It's our right field and first-base combination. I had a couple of ways to go against Phil Niekro.

(1) Play Art Shamsky at first base and use Swoboda in right field, or...

(2) Play Shamsky in right field and use either Ed Kranepool or Donn Clendenon at first base.

In other words, Shamsky was going to play. I had to make up my mind if I wanted Swoboda or Clendenon or Kranepool in the lineup.

Mets Best

October 4, 1969
by Casey Stengel

Let's get one thing straight at the start. The Mets I think will play all the way to the end of the World Series because they have more pitchers and they throw lightning. And you can look it up, that's best for a short series.

Both these clubs is the greatest in the league. They got winning streaks that go 10 straight and yesterday don't count. Both clubs is in good condition but Seaver is the youngest, he was born in 1944 or some year like that.

Let's talk about the managers. They are two of the youngest that are well-experienced. Both are the greatest, absolutely amazin' that Hodges has more experience.

They got Aaron that's the best all-time ball player at the present time. I was in St. Louis for an old-timers game and I seen him win the most games against St. Louis, and Cepeda won the other always at the end of the game.

Don't forget, I say it goes the limit to the World Series for the Mets.

Mets' 5-Run 8th Takes Opener, 9-5

by Phil Pepe

T he Mets, who won seven games more than any other National League team, beat the Braves eight out of 12 during the regular season and handled Atlanta ace Phil Niedro three-for-three, were forced to do it again for the disbelievers as they met the Braves in the opener of the NL's first scheduled championship playoff series here today.

The Mets won 9-5.

But to convince the skeptics was 24-year-old Met right-hander Tom Seaver, the major's leading winner with a 25-7 record and victories in three games over the Braves in three decisions during the regular season.

The Braves contend—and the oddsmakers concur—that it's a brand new season—that what happened before is past and that they are a new team with the confidence of winners and the momentum of a 17-out-of-21 streak in the stretch.

The Mets maintained a confident. "We did it before and we can do it again" attitude.

They have defied the oddsmakers all season, winning the NL East as 100-1 underdogs, and manager Gil Hodges remained confident. His prediction: "The Mets within five games."

A capacity crowd of 50,000 was on hand in perfect baseball weather, clear and sunny with the temperature in the 80s and a slight breeze blowing from left field to right. ■

Mets pitcher Tom Seaver hugs catcher J. C. Martin after the Mets won the opening game of the NLCS.

Mets Outlast Braves, Go for Sweep Today

by Phil Pepe

Confounding the experts and pounding the Braves' pitchers for the second straight day, the Mets used their bats to club out an 11-6 victory here today and take a commanding 2-0 lead in the best-of-five playoff series to determine that NL champion.

DAILY NEWS   John Duprey

A crowd of 50,270 fans looked on in disbelief as the usually good-pitch weak-hit Mets pounded six Atlanta pitchers for 13 hits, including home runs by Ken Boswell, Tommie Agee and Cleon Jones. Jones also had a single and double and three RBI. Art Shamsky chipped in with three singles, and Agee and Wayne Garrett had two hits each. The Braves kicked in with three errors and generally shoddy play in the field.

The Mets needed all the support they got on a day when Jerry Koosman did not have his best stuff. The Braves chased him with a five-run fifth and Ron Taylor had to come in to stem the tide. Taylor pitched a scoreless sixth to get credit for the victory. Tug McGraw worked the last three innings and put down a ninth inning Braves' uprising to preserve the victory. ■

A pro-Met banner cheers on pitcher Jerry Koosman. Koosman left after the fifth inning. Ron Taylor got the win and Tug McGraw pitched the final three innings.

N L C S ' 6 9

Nuts to 4 p.m. start

Casey Stengel Playoff Report

by Casey Stengel

They should never change the game like this. This here 4 o'clock start is twilight baseball that's what it is and don't you think it doesn't change the game.

They wouldn't do it in the World Series, would they? Around here baseball's coming back, it was once football country the last 10 years. They're gonna have to play a little earlier and forget the football game.

When I was a player which I was 15, 20 years once, I was a sun fielder—not an outfielder. Let me tell you there's a difference. Now you take that center fielder Agee which he plays along with Jones. This time of year playin' twilight baseball like this it's important like Agee says he can feel Jones near him when they go for a ball.

Well, Sir, let me tell you with that low sun sittin' on the roof of this here ballpark you can't play the hitters you gotta play the sun. When they start ball games normal like the sun's way up there and you can turn away from it to see the ball come up at you. ■

DAILY NEWS   John Duprey

Cleon Jones almost took off Tommie Agee's head with a foul ball.

Agee Almost Lost His Head

October 6, 1969
by Wes Gaffer

Tommie Agee almost lost his head in the seventh inning. That's when he broke for home with Cleon Jones at bat. He dropped into his slide as Jones made contact with the pitch and lined it foul.

"Damn, the ball just grazed my head," Agee said as he stripped off his undershirt in the clubhouse. "No, there was no sign. I was on my own."

Jones, who lined a Cecil Upshaw pitch into the stands in left before Agee had time to regain his breath, shook his head. "I didn't see him but I heard him coming and I saw the pitcher speed up his windup.

"I didn't want to hit the ball; just swinging to keep the catcher occupied, just a flick of the bat like this," and he gave his wrist a little snap.

The NL Pennant Flies at Shea

by Phil Pepe

n only the eighth year of their existence and in the first year of divisional play, the Mets are champs. Not ersatz champions of a division, but champs of the whole National League. All of it, from New York to Chicago to St. Louis to Los Angeles.

Amazing. Incredible. Stupendous. Unbelievable. Fantastic. Terrific. Magnificent. The Mets are all of those and more. They are champions and, as the man said, "You ain't seen nothing yet." Yesterday the National League, tomorrow the world.

The glorious climax came at 3:34 p.m. yesterday as Wayne Garrett threw out Tony Gonzalez, and when the ball settled in the glove of first baseman Eddie Kranepool, it was over. The Mets had beaten the Braves, 7-4, had swept them in the best three-of-five playoff series, had won the National League pennant.

Again, it touched off a wild celebration from the fans, not as wild and not as destructive as the night they won the Eastern Division because this was largely a World Series crowd, and more than half of the 53,195 fans were businessmen.

But there were the kids, the long-suffering kids. Always with the Mets there are the kids. They had made this their own holiday from school and they had come to celebrate. Again, they mobbed their heroes and tore up the field and swiped every base and this time they didn't miss first base.

It was a championship that had to be earned. The Mets had won 100 games, more than any other team in the National League, but, it wasn't enough. Now they had to prove it all over again. Now they had to beat the Braves three out of five, and, if they didn't, those 100 games and that division title would have been hollow victories. The frustration and the disappointment would have been intolerable.

But the Mets had not disappointed their fans all year and they didn't disappoint them this time. They beat the Braves and in a sweep, no less. They beat them with the dispatch and facility of the old Yankee teams. They beat them today with three home runs—by Ken Boswell, Tommie Agee and Wayne Garrett—and with 14 hits off three Braves' pitchers, who must be shell-shocked by now.

That made 27 runs and 37 hits in three pressure, championship games from a team that had a reputation of being unfair to the lumber industry.

Pitching, everybody said. The Mets would beat you with their pitching and everybody thought that meant Tom Seaver and Jerry Koosman and Gary Gentry, but it also meant Tug McGraw and Ron Taylor—and yesterday it meant Nolan Ryan.

It was Nolan Ryan who did it. Nolan Ryan, who throws bee-bees and who had suffered through a year of disappointment because of injuries and service absences. Nolan Ryan, who had not thrown a ball in combat during the first two games and two innings of the third.

Henry Aaron had bombed his third playoff homer with Tony Gonzalez on in the first to give the Braves a 2-0 lead and Gonzales had singled and Aaron had doubled him to third with none out in the third. It was nervous time as Gentry went 1-2 on Rico Carty. On the next pitch, Carty whistled a vicious, foul line drive into the leftfield stands and Gil Hodges came out to the mound and it was the first time a pitcher was knocked out by a foul ball.

Ryan came in and blew his fastball by Carty. That's one. Orlando Cepeda was put on to load them and Ryan blew a third-strike fastball by Clete Boyer, a fastball so swift that Clete never got his bat off his shoulder. That's two.

Rookie Bob Didier battled Ryan's smoke, finally lining to left. The Braves were out without scoring and you knew that the Mets could do it, the 53,195 fans knew the Mets could do it, the Mets knew the Mets could do it, and even the Braves knew the Mets could do it.

Agee's homer over the centerfield wall cut it to 2-1 in the third and in the next inning, the Mets were ahead. Again they used their newfound long-ball

Tommie Agee drives a first-inning double in Game 3 of the NLCS.

power, as Boswell homered into the rightfield bullpen behind Art Shamsky's single, and the Mets led, 3-2.

But the Braves had just enough fight left to take the lead one more time in the fifth. Ryan got in trouble the only way Ryan can get in trouble, he walked Carty with one out. Then Cepeda saw Nolan's fastball well enough to hit it downtown, over the 396 sign in left center and the Braves led, 4-3.

It was the last of the fifth and the Mets were one run down and, with Ryan leading off, Gil Hodges might have gone for a pinch-hitter and a fresh pitcher for the sixth. But he let Ryan bat and Nolan stroked a single to right, and who's going to second-guess Gil Hodges?

Then came Garrett and miracles were still very much in vogue.

Garrett hit Jarvis' first pitch into the second deck, just inside the right foul pole and the Mets were ahead, 5-4, in this science-fiction piece, this series of the occult. Cleon Jones followed with a double to Pat Jarvis and it became 6-4 when Boswell singled home his third run of the game.

Later, they got one more run on Jerry Grote's double and Agee's single, but Ryan didn't need it. Not this day. Not this week. Not this year.

"We're the greatest team in the world right now," Cleon Jones was saying, while the fans were still taking their souvenirs. ■

Mets catcher Jerry Grote hugs winner Nolan Ryan. Ryan went seven innings in relief of Gary Gentry.

They Tore It up for Mets; But Shea Survives

by Norm Miller

Groundskeepers go back to work today repairing the second holocaust of Shea Stadium.

Within seconds of the final out in the Mets' historic pennant clincher yesterday, thousands of delirious fans ignored a plea from the management and poured out onto the field in a wild mob scene.

This one was not quite as destructive as the night of the September 24 pennant-clincher, but it did nothing to improve the topography of the beautiful ballpark where the World Series will be played next Tuesday.

As the Braves batted in the eighth, and the Mets' clincher became imminent, young fans in droves made their way from the upper stands and swarmed down the aisles toward the lower field boxes.

Came the plea over the public address system by announcer Jack Lightcap:

"Ladies and gentlemen, boys and girls. We ask your cooperation in not going on the playing field at the conclusion of the game. We are hoping for a Met appearance in the World Series and urge you to consider the condition of the field. Should we reach our greatest triumph by qualifying for the World Series, it is imperative that the field be in the best possible condition…"

The rest of the announcement was drowned out in a chorus of boos. The management might just as well have spared the voltage for the speaker system.

Luckily, no injuries were reported.

Cops, badly outnumbered, did their best to disperse the frolicking kids. It was slow progress. Eventually, perhaps a half-hour later, they departed in their own good time.

Moral of this story: Today was no day to tell a Met fan where he can or cannot go. Today is his day too. ∎

DAILY NEWS John Duprey

NL pennant-winning Mets Jerry Grote and Rod Gaspar give New York Mayor John Lindsay a champagne bath.

DAILY NEWS   Gene Kappock

Ed Kranepool &
Donn Clendenon

Krane Got 85G to Sign;
Donn Was Fed Peanuts

by Dick Young

When Ed Kranepool was 17, the Mets gave him $85,000 to become a professional ballplayer. When Donn Clendenon was 21, the Pirates gave him $500. This indicates that Kranepool was a better first baseman than Clendenon, or a better businessman, or merely that Branch Rickey was a more persuasive talker than anybody the Mets had.

"I didn't like baseball when I was a kid," says Donn Clendenon. "I liked football and basketball better."

His father had died when Donn was three months, and when he was three years his mother married Nish Williams. Fans of the old Negro leagues will know that name. He was an outstanding catcher who played with Roy Campanella. When Donn Clendenon speaks of his father, he means Nish Williams.

"He told me I should play all sports, and when I didn't play baseball he'd take away my allowance, and the keys to the car," says Donn Clendenon. He would have been a professional football player, a wide receiver, if he hadn't injured his knee after graduating Morehouse College. He had tryout offers from the Browns, Skins and Eagles, he says, but somewhere along the line Branch Rickey showed up in Atlanta to speak to the 100% Wrong Club. Branch Rickey had Jackie Robinson with him. Between the two of them, Donn Clendenon was a pushover. He signed for "five or six hundred," he remembers, "and a contract for $300 a month in D-ball."

Donn Clendenon has come a long way. He made the Pirates in '61, knocked in a lot of runs for them for eight years, became the cause celebre in an expansion transfer of bodies, and wound up, June 15, in New York. The Mets figured they were getting a righty long-baller, possibly to platoon with Ed Kranepool at first base. They also were getting a conglomerate.

Donn Clendenon, in addition to signing a $50,000 baseball contract for 1969, is the owner of a posh new duplex dinner club in Atlanta, vice-president of the Scripto Co. there; a director of Diplomat Corp.

Ed Kranepool, in addition to first-basing for the Mets, is a customer's man on Wall St. and owns a piece of the Sayonara Motel on Long Island. Considering the men who play first base at Shea, it is possible that if you lift the bag you will find gold buried there.

Ed Kranepool is the youngest old man in baseball. He has seven years in the majors at age 24. That's seven equity years in the players' pension plan, in case his other interests don't pan out.

"Funny," says Ed Kranepool about his senior citizen status, "but I feel good when a kid on the club comes up to me and asks how to hit certain pitchers. I feel I'm contributing something, even if I'm not playing. I used to sulk when I wasn't playing."

Ed Kranepool is a complexity of appreciation and resentment at this stage. He is grateful that the Mets did not trade him, and yet, if he had it all to do over, Ed Kranepool doubts seriously he would join the original Mets.

"I think I'd sign with a better ballclub, not a new franchise," he says. "The frustration of six years took a lot out of me. I was part of a joke. That drains you. You lose your desire. Even if you had a great day, say 4-for-4, the team probably wound up losing and you felt lousy."

Tips on Cutoff

The cutoff is designed to prevent the man who has singled from taking an extra base when the out fielder throws to the plate. Let's say the single goes to right and the man on second heads home. You line up the throw, trying to get to within 10 or 15 feet of home. Then, as the throw comes in, you run towards it. If the catcher yells to let it go, you do, but you still give the decoy wave at the ball to make the coach hold the man at first.

—Ed Kranepool

"REACH!"   —By Bill Gallo

World Series

'69

Facing an Orioles team that matched up better than the Mets in almost every category on paper, even New Yorkers might have had their doubts.

Any such doubts turned into reality in the opening game, when 25-game winner Tom Seaver got roughed up in a 4-1 loss.

The Mets magic was back the next day as Jerry Koosman took a no-hitter into the seventh inning and gave up just two hits as the Mets won 2-1 on Donn Clendenon's solo shot to right field and an Al Weis RBI single. The Series shifted back to New York for the next three games.

With famous New Yorkers Joe DiMaggio and Jacqueline Onassis on hand, how could the Mets disappoint? One man who wouldn't disappoint was Tommie Agee. Not only did he drive one into the stands in the first inning, he also made a pair of spectacular catches that deprived the Orioles of five runs as the Mets went up a game.

It was Ron Swoboda who sent the fourth game of the Series to extra innings with his diving catch in the ninth inning, and when Rod Gaspar scored the winning run in extra innings, the Mets were just a game away from the World Championship.

Mets Could End War in 3 Days: Richards

by Dick Young

**P**aul Richards congratulated Gil Hodges for winning the NL pennant, both parts; and came out of the room shaking his head. "You could send the Mets to Vietnam," he said, "and they'd end it in three days."

Paul Richards is the GM, the man who put the Braves together, before the Mets took them apart in three days. He is considered something of a baseball brain, at all levels. He built teams, good teams, in Baltimore, in Houston and in Atlanta. He managed. As a player, he was a smart catcher. He had to be, with his bat. But this time, he didn't have the answer.

"I don't know," he said. "I just don't know. How can we shell their three starting pitchers the way we did, and hardly be in any of the three games. I can't figure it. I can't."

Try. ∎

We'll Beat Orioles 4 Straight, Says Jubilant Jones

October 7, 1969
by Wes Gaffer

Drenched in champagne, dripping sweat but not caring, Cleon Jones yelled, "We're gonna beat Baltimore in four straight, then I'm going fishing."

"Nobody's gonna stop us," he roared, trying to pierce the roaring underground that was the Mets' clubhouse following the three-game sweep of the Braves. "I just got me a brand new boat and I can hardly wait to get it on the Spanish River in Mobile."

Ron Taylor, who contributed two fine relief jobs to the sweep, was standing quietly out of the way. "In all of this, don't forget the man responsible for it—Gil Hodges. He's been just wonderful all year, patient with us; that's his secret, patience. What a wonderful guy."

The wonderful guy theme was echoed by plate umpire Ed Sudol, who had an opportunity to test Hodges' patience early in the game when catcher Jerry Grote and Hodges protested a checked swing call, "Let me tell you," he said in the tunnel leading to the umps' dressing room, "this is a fine man. Hodges taught these kids patience."

Gil Maps pre-WS Program;
Casey Sees a Sweep

October 7, 1969
by Gil Hodges

The Mets are the champions of the National League. Let me think about that for a while. I think that's just wonderful, don't you? The only thing that could be more wonderful might just happen next week.

If anybody had told you this was going to be a hitters' series, this NL playoff, you'd have said, then Atlanta will win it. Be honest. You would, wouldn't you? I would.

These hitters showed me something. I know we had some good hitters, but they still showed me something. This playoff series was very, very important for that reason. It brought the Met hitters the appreciation they deserve, the recognition they haven't been getting. And now, the Orioles must worry about our hitting as well as our pitching.

October 7, 1969
by Casey Stengel

The World Series in four straight? I don't see why not. I tole' ya at the beginning of this here thing that when you're goofed up like these here fellers is what's goin' to stop 'em. They don't have to see that Aaron because it's a long winter.

They haven't missed have they? We have beaten the best what is in the National League in September. Why should they stop playing bad now which they are hitting harder than ever they ever hit.

These young fellers ain't had no slump being they beat this club in three straight, why can't they win in Baltimore? Baltimore played 12, 11 innings and these fellers with what with all those young arms which hasn't had to go to sleep yet they can throw all day and night.

I tell you, the way these young men is hitting they built the ballpark too small it takes 'em too long to play the game. I think they're going to move the fences back.

DAILY NEWS

Casey Stengel, Daily News correspondent, at the '69 World Series.

Gil Switches to Donn, Ron against Bird Lefties

by Phil Pepe

Unlike their Eastern Division championship, the Mets' victory over the Braves for the NL pennant was not a team effort. The Mets needed only 17 players to sweep the Braves, and if they can beat the Braves with 17 players, why can't they beat the Orioles with 25?

Eight Mets saw no action at all against the Braves—Ron Swoboda, Donn Clendenon, Duffy Dyer, Ed Charles and pitchers Cal Koonce and Jack DiLauro, Don Cardwell, Jim McAndrew. The vacation is about to come to an end for at least two of the eight.

Against the Orioles, Clendenon and Swoboda suddenly become key Mets because the first two Baltimore pitchers are left-handers—Mike Cuellar and Dave McNally. Against them, Clendenon will replace Ed Kranepool at first and Swoboda will sub for Art Shamsky in right. The changes do not weaken the Mets either offensively or defensively.

Bench and bullpen have been a critical part of the Mets' success all season, so it was no surprise when in the third game against the Braves, Nolan Ryan struck a blow in behalf of the second-line pitching.

Former Yankee teammates Joe DiMaggio and Yogi Berra get re-acquainted as the World Series moved to Shea Stadium.

While everybody was looking for Tom Seaver, Jerry Koosman and Gary Gentry to dazzle the Braves, along came Tug McGraw, Ron Taylor and Nolan Ryan to deliver the haymaker. But then nobody ever said this was a three-man pitching staff, although only six men were used in the playoffs. ■

world series '69

Logic Picks Orioles to Win

by Red Foley

**U**ntil somebody, be he M. Donald Grant, C. Dillon Stengel or Mandrake the Magician, measures the amount of Cinderella in the Mets, it says here that Baltimore's obstinate Orioles are the one team the Amazins can't beat.

The AL champions, as they proved during the season and again in the Divisionals, can do it all. They win with pitching, power and defense. They can win with finesse, they can do it with force. The Orioles aren't lucky. They're good.

But are they good enough to stop a club that of late has done nothing but win? The logical answer is yes. But when were logic and the Mets an entry? Will the Amazin' Ones win the World Series? No. Can they win the World Series? Yes.

Confusing, isn't it? That's because the answer cannot be contained in comparisons and matchups. The Mets, who once defied description, now defy logic.

It's their Cinderella dimensions that do it. Measure that and you'll know it all. Are the Mets a team of destiny? The Orioles don't think so.

"We're Number One" was their chant following the three-game wipeout of a competent Minnesota club. The Orioles are the best balanced ballclub since the '61 Yankees. ∎

Mets' Success Foils Jets

October 7, 1969
by Larry Fox

Now the New York Orphans are having trouble finding a home away from home. With the Mets yesterday clinching the National League pennant, it appears a certainty that their third scheduled "home" game will have to be switched to Houston's Astrodome.

But wait a minute. The Oilers, it has been learned, aren't overwhelming the homeless Jets with southern hospitality. They don't relish the thought of playing their top rivals for the Eastern championship in Shea Stadium on Dec. 6. Both teams, of course, would be playing in any snow or freezing weather, but the advantage would go to the team that happened to be used to it.

world series '69

Gil Sticks to Rotation

by Gil Hodges

The Mets' pitching plans for the World Series are these: Seaver, Koosman and Gentry.

Sounds familiar? That's right, we're going the same way we did in the play-offs. I know some people think we should start Nolan Ryan because of the great job he did for us in the last game of the playoffs. They think you should just write off Gary Gentry because he didn't have a good game.

If you're going to do that, then you'd have to write off Seaver and Koosman, too. A manager doesn't operate that way.

We can look for much better pitching in the World Series. It has to be, knowing what these boys have done and can do. I just hope our hitting continues. It is pleasant to watch.

That brings me to our lineup against Baltimore. The Orioles have lefty starters, something the Braves didn't throw at us. When they use left-handers like Mike Cuellar and Dave McNally, we'll counterattack with our big right-handed hitters:

Donn Clendenon will play first base.
Ron Swoboda will play right field.
Ed Charles will play third base.
Al Weis will play second base.

That's the way we've been doing it, and it has worked. But I don't want you to hold me to it 100%.

Orioles manager Earl Weaver and Mets manager Gil Hodges share a moment before the World Series gets under way.

That's the look ahead. Now, the look backward; the pleasant, fond look backward. People ask me, very often, to pick out a day, a time, when the Mets suddenly became winners, when everything turned around. I don't believe you can pick a specific day or event, or game, but I can single out a feeling.

The Mets became winners when they began believing they could win. I think the Mets are an outstanding example of what a wonderful thing confidence is within yourself.

That is the long look backward. Now, we look only ahead. ∎

w o r l d   s e r i e s   ' 6 9

Mets Outclassed, so May Need 5 to Win

by Phil Pepe

If you had any doubts about it, here's a rundown of how the Orioles have it all over the Mets on a position-by-position basis:

FIRST BASE—Powell is big enough, strong enough and mean enough to make pitchers wish they had gone to med school. Clendenon and Kranepool are no match whether hitting, fielding, arm wrestling or in a dark alley.

Edge: Orioles.

SECOND BASE—Another platoon spot for Mets, another strong one for Birds. Johnson can outfield Boswell and out hit Weis.

SHORTSTOP—Birds' Belanger considered finest glove man in AL. Harrelson is considered best in NL. But Belanger doesn't play fair. He went and upped his BA more than 80 points to .287 and his RBI to 51 and the "out man" isn't an out man anymore.

Edge: Orioles.

THIRD BASE—No contest. Brooks Robinson is a longtime star, a close competitor of Pie Traynor for all-time third baseman. Mets will platoon Charles, who didn't even make it as Kansas City's all-time third sacker, and Garrett.

Edge: Orioles.

LEFTFIELD—The Mets may find they can run on Buford's arm, but he has good speed and a switch at bat that hit .291 with 11 homers. Jones batted almost 50 points higher, can match Buford in power, speed and defense.

Edge: Mets.

CENTERFIELD—Not much to choose on power and run production. Both Agee and Blair have

26 HRs, 76 RBI. But the Bird has the edge, albeit a slight one, in speed, arm, defense and average.

Edge: Orioles.

RIGHTFIELD—There's very little to choose between Frank Robinson and Hank Aaron.

Edge: Orioles.

CATCHER—This is where the Birds platoon—Etchebarren vs. lefties, Hendricks vs. righties. For the Mets, it's Grote, probably against everybody.

Edge: Mets.

PITCHING—If the Mets don't have it here, they don't have it anywhere. Throw out the poor playoff performances of Seaver, Koosman and Gentry. Nerves, they say. Tom and Jerry haven't had two bad games back-to-back all year—why now? The Mets beat Cuellar in the NL and have beaten better pitchers than McNally and Palmer. Mets second line pitching of Ryan, McAndrew and Cardwell is good enough to start anywhere else.

Edge: Mets.

BULLPEN—Taylor and McGraw are outstanding relievers, but the Birds can double up on them with four good ones. Lopez and Richert can smoke against lefties, Watt and Hall are tough against anyone.

Edge: Orioles.

BENCH—The Mets' bench strength is in their platooning. But for pinch-hitting, their record is poor.

Edge: Orioles.

Surprise: Orioles Staff Has Better ERA Than Mets

by Joe Trimble

hat's all this stuff about the Mets having a big chance to beat the Orioles because their pitching is superior? We'll win with Seaver and Kooz and order more booze! Well, the Birds didn't win 109 games without some pretty fine arms.

Two of their three starters were second and third in the AL behind ERA leader Dick Bosman of Washington. Mike Cuellar, who works the opener Saturday in Baltimore, was third with 2.38 and Jim Palmer, who opens at Shea in the third game Tuesday, was runner-up with 2.34.

The ERA for the entire staff was a remarkably low 2.83. The Mets' hurlers had a combined 2.99.

"I hear the Mets have six good pitchers," Bird boss Earl Weaver said yesterday. "Well, we've got 10."

Of his 10, two had extensive careers in the NL and opposed the Mets as late as last year—Cuellar and reliever Dick Hall. The 32-year-old lefthander was 0-2 against Gil Hodges' group last season and is 5-5 lifetime with a 2.64 ERA.

The Cuban was with the Cardinals in 1964 and the Astros from 1965-68. In 16 games against the

NLCS Game 3 winner Nolan Ryan makes sure he's ready to go in the World Series.

Metsies, nine of them starts, he hurled 75 1/3 innings. In 72 rounds over his last four NL seasons, he has not yielded a homer to them. ■

DAILY NEWS John Duprey

world series '69

... And Now for That Other Miracle

by Joe Trimble

This is the year of the bird, according to the Chinese calendar. Baltimore, which hardly could be confused with Hong Kong, has adopted that reference as its slogan for the 66th World Series, between its brilliant Orioles and the Amazin' Mets.

The Orioles open with their big winner, left handed Mike Cuellar (23-11 and 2.41 ERA) and the Mets with Tom Seaver, the top pitcher in both leagues (25-7 and 2.21 ERA).

Surprisingly, there may be some empty seats. As of this morning, over 2,000 were still available. They were put on sale with the purchaser obliged to buy tickets for at least two games, either Nos. 1 and 7 or Nos. 2 and 6. Most of those remaining are obstructed views and were not marked.

Chances are they won't all be taken because the games may be more attractive on color-TV than from behind a pole.

The Mets, few of whom ever playcd here, took over at 1:30 p.m. to familiarize themselves with the ballpark.

"It looks like a pitcher's park," Seaver said. ■

Jacqueline Kennedy Onassis with husband Aristotle and children John Jr. and Caroline.

world series '69

Oriole Fans Size Up Mets
"We'll Beat 'em 4 Straight"

by Phil Pepe

When the Mets took the field for their day-before-the-game workout, members of the local press stood and gawked in disbelief. Yes, the Mets really do exist. No, they are no robots, they are human-type people. No, they are not figments of the overactive imagination of some fiction writer, they only play that way.

world series '69

The people of Baltimore don't believe the Mets just like they didn't believe the Jets and they didn't believe the Knicks. The cab driver said that was different. The cab driver said, "We'll beat them four straight."

"We're going to sock it to them," said Blaze Starr, Yes, that Blaze Starr, Baltimore's No. 1 figure, its leading natural resource.

On the Mets' bus heading for the workout at Municipal Stadium, Tom Seaver picked up a local newspaper. "Do you call this objective reporting?" asked the pitcher, a student of journalism and opposing hitters. The headline said: "Miracle of Mets Near End."

> "What does that mean? We haven't played a game and it sounds like we're behind, 3-0. "
>
> —Tom Seaver

"What does that mean?" Seaver asked. "We haven't played a game and it sounds like we're behind, 3-0."

The Mets are behind. They're behind in hitting, fielding, pitching, running and betting. But they haven't lost. Not yet they haven't.

The answer is simple. The people who work for New York papers have seen and they believe. With the Mets, there is no believing without seeing. And that is the charm and the hidden weapon of the Mets. Overconfidence can cost the Orioles this Series and the people of Baltimore their psyches. Overconfidence already cost the rest of the NL a pennant. ∎

Series Opener Is for the Birds, 4-1

by Joe Trimble

The Brilliant Birds bombed Tom Seaver, the winningest pitcher in baseball, this afternoon to mess up the Mets, 4-1, in the opening game of the 66th World Series. The New York ace lasted only five innings and allowed all six Baltimore hits.

Mike Cuellar, the Cuban left-hander, went the distance and also doled out six hits. He struck out eight and walked four. The Mets' run came on a sacrifice fly in the seventh after the AL champs had scored their four.

However, the star of the day for the 50,429 fans—short of capacity by more than 2,000—was Brooks Robinson, the unbelievable third baseman. He made six tremendous plays to keep Cuellar in the game.

The incomparable fielder simply took the game away from the Mets with his golden glove. He has been voted the finest fielder at his position by the AL players for nine straight years and will be again. Off today's great play, the Mets will vote for him, too.

The Mets' run, incidentally, ended a string of 38 scoreless innings in World Series play by the Orioles, who swept the Dodgers in 1966, with the final three games being shutouts. They are the only team to have never lost a Series game.

Strangely, the Orioles won without any offensive help from their three power hitters in the middle of the batting order. Frank Robinson was blanked, as was Brooks, while Boog Powell had only a single that didn't affect the result. Don Buford got the Birds

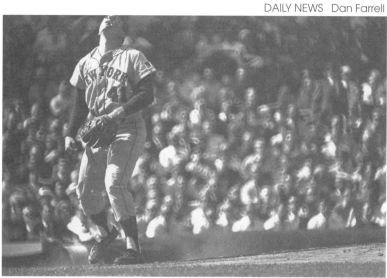

DAILY NEWS Dan Farrell

Tom Seaver watches Don Buford's leadoff home run sail out of the park in Game 1 of the World Series.

off swinging with a leadoff home run in the opening inning.

"I had good stuff for 3 2/3 innings and then lost it," Seaver said.

Tom had won 25 games in the regular season, the final 10 in succession, then the playoff opener against Atlanta. Cuellar, a 32-year-old screwballer picked up from Houston in the off season, won 23 and finished fast with 13 victories in his last 16 decisions. ∎

Mets Gotta Be Better; Brooks' Glove Awes Amazins

by Red Foley

Brooks Robinson, the guy with the big hands, and Earl Weaver, the one with the big mouth, were doing most of the talking in the Orioles' dressing room today. Don Buford and Mike Cuellar were also supplying a share of the chin music, but neither attracted as large an audience as the other two.

Weaver, a charming guy and a very capable manager, has the unhappy faculty of sometimes saying the right thing at the wrong time.

"They're about what we expected," Weaver said. Then he added a postscript that could turn the Mets on. "Of course they have to have more than they showed us today. They must have something because they did win 100 games in that big, beautiful National League, didn't they?"

"That's going to look awful sarcastic when it comes out in the papers," a Baltimore writer said. "I know it," Weaver replied, a sheepish look on his face. "But it's true they did win 100 games, so they must be better than they were today." ∎

world series '69

Ron Swoboda slumps against the rightfield fence after a leap that failed to prevent Don Buford's first-inning home run in Game 1.

It's Even! Kooz, Ron 2-Hit Birds, 2-1

by Joe Trimble

The Mets are alive, fairly well and just about breathing. In a taut, tension-filled thriller, they beat the Orioles in the ninth today, 2-1, to even the 66th World Series at a game apiece. It was a brilliant battle of excellent pitching and great defenses, which left the 50,850 fans shaking.

For the first time, the Birds had lost a World Series game. However, they didn't go down until a furious finishing effort fell just short.

Jerry Koosman, who hurled a two-hitter, walked himself out of the drama after two outs in the ninth with passes to Frank Robinson and Boog Powell on 3-2 counts. Reliever Ron Taylor relieved him and went the full number again with the toughest clutch player on the Baltimore club, Brooks Robinson.

Brooks then rammed a hard grounder at Ed Charles, the Met third baseman. With the maximum count on the batter, the runners were flying on the bases. Merv Rettenmund, who had gone in with young legs to run for Frank Robby, flew into third as Charles muffled the ball against his chest.

Ed started to run to third for the force and sensed that the kid would beat him. So, he stopped and threw to first base. The toss was low but long Donn Clendenon reached for it with one hand just before it hit the ground and held it for the most important third out in the 1,296 games this team has played in eight giddy years of existence.

This game had it all. Koosman, the 25-year-old left-hander, had a no-hitter through six innings. Paul Blair broke it up with a clean single in the seventh and went on to score the tying run.

Clendenon had gained the lead for New York in the fourth with a homer to right field against Dave McNally, 26-year-old southpaw who had pitched 24 consecutive scoreless innings in post-season play, a nine-inning shutout of the Dodgers in the final game of the 1966 World Series, 12 in the second playoff game this year against the Twins and the first three today. ■

DAILY NEWS Dan Farrell

Jerry Koosman evened the World Series at one game apiece.

In addition to the great pitching and fielding, this game marked the first time in series history that a team had played four outfielders.

Manager Gil Hodges startled the fans here and the TV millions by sending second baseman Weis into left field when Frank Robinson came up in the ninth. It is a play he uses only against long-ball hitters when he is leading by a run or tied in the last inning.

Until his control cracked in the final phase, Koosman was magnificent. But after the pair of two-out walks, Gil could not leave him in to face Brooks, who had driven in the tying run in the seventh. ■

The winning hit blurs off the bat of Al Weis in the ninth inning of Game 2 of the World Series.

Gil on His 4 Outfielders

October 12, 1969
by Gil Hodges

I'll try to explain why we used the four outfielders against Frank Robinson with two out in the ninth inning. There is a very valid baseball reason. We are trying to shut off the extra-base alleys.

First I would like to say it is nothing unusual. The Mets have used it against other hitters of this type, men like Richie Allen and Willie McCovey, men who can hurt you with the extra-base hit. Other teams do it, too, when the right occasion arises.

We are not trying to tempt the hitter, or taunt him. We are trying simply to keep the man from getting an extra base hit. I mean a double or triple. If a hitter of this calibre wants to settle for a single by going for the wide open hole on the right side of the infield, let him. We'll give it to him. It still takes two more singles to get the run in. If he gets a double, it takes only one more hit.

I have been asked, why don't we simply throw four bad pitches and walk him? To that, I say there's always a chance of getting him out, like we did the first three times today, when he hit the ball rather well.

Agee Whiz! Mets Go 1 Up in Series

by Phil Pepe

A city that has seen Joe DiMaggio and Willie Mays play centerfield—and figured it had seen it all—now has seen Tommie Agee. Not once, but twice. Agee went to his right, then went to his left, and came up with a pair of spectacular catches that will rank among the greatest in World Series history.

The two catches saved the Mets five runs, exactly their margin of victory as they blanked the Orioles, 5-0, in Shea yesterday and took a 2-1 lead in the best-of-seven Series to crown baseball's 1969 World Champion. With their aces, Tom Seaver and Jerry Koosman, ready to pitch games four and five, the Mets figure they can wrap it up in five and avoid a return trip to Baltimore.

Rookie right-hander Gary Gentry, just a week past his 23d birthday, got credit for the victory with saves going to Nolan Ryan and Agee. Gentry departed with the bags loaded and two out in the seventh, and Ryan came in to wrap up the four-hit shutout.

It was obvious this would be Agee's day right from the start. After Gentry retired the Orioles in the first, Tommie led off for the Mets and drilled Jim Palmer's 2-1 fastball over the center wall. It was his first hit in the series and emphasized the reason manager Gil Hodges likes to have Agee leading off. It's an old Casey Stengel idea, hoping to grab a psychological advantage with a big hit to start the game.

Gary's big blast came after Jerry Grote walked and Bud Harrelson singled with two out. Then Gentry jumped on Palmer's pitch, a high fastball that landed at the start of the warning track some 10 feet

Tommie Agee makes his second dramatic catch in Game 3 of the World Series.

Tommie Agee made one of the greatest catches in World Series history in the fourth inning.

in front of the 396-foot sign slightly to the right of center. The hit was Gentry's first since August 3. He had failed to hit in his last 28 at-bats and had driven in one run all year.

Playing Hendricks to pull in the fourth inning, Agee was over in right-center and deep, but Ellie crossed him up by hitting the ball hard the other way. With the crack of the bat, everybody was running—Agee to left-center and the two Oriole baserunners tearing around the infield.

After going full speed for about 40 yards, Tommie caught up with the ball near the fence, reached out backhanded and caught the ball in the webbing of his glove about waist high. It was a catch that veteran press box observers were rating over Mays' back-to-the-plate grab of Vic Wertz' drive in the 1954 Series. Al Gionfriddo's steal against Joe DiMaggio in the 1947 Series and Sandy Amoros' one-hand grab of Yogi Berra's opposite-field shot in the 1955 Series.

It was a catch that electrified the crowd of 56,335, including the distinguished gray-haired

gentleman sitting in Commissioner Bowie Kuhn's box to the left of the Mets' dugout. The man's name is Joe DiMaggio.

It was a catch that Agee almost didn't make. "The ball," he said, "almost went through my webbing."

It was a catch that saved at least two runs and protected the Mets' 3-0 lead.

It was a catch that brought the inevitable press box crack, "I'd like to see him do it again," a parody of a line Charlie Dressen once delivered after Willie Mays made one of his unbelievable grabs against the Dodgers. In this case, the quipster had to wait just three more innings to see Agee do it again.

The Mets upped their lead to 4-0 in the sixth, when Grote cracked a double to left to deliver Ken Boswell, who had singled and moved to second as Ed Kranepool grounded out to the right side.

Gentry was still firing zips when the Birds came to bat in the seventh. Hendricks drove deep to center and Davey Johnson did likewise. Then, with two out and nobody on, Gentry was bitten by wildness. He failed to find the plate against Mark Belanger. He also walked pinch-looker Dave May, then loaded the bases by throwing four off the plate to Don Buford.

With Blair, the tying run, coming to bat and Gentry obviously tiring, Hodges reached into his pen for smoke-thrower Nolan Ryan, the 22-year-old right-hander who was the hero of the third playoff game against the Braves.

Everybody in the park knew what Ryan was going to do—throw bullets. Blair looked at the first lightning bolt, then swung and missed at the second lightning bolt. Now the Mets were one strike away from getting out of the inning.

But Blair hit the next fastball and it went out faster than it had come in, heading for the alley in right-center. Three runners took off and so did Tommie Agee.

This time he didn't have to run very far. This time he did not have to reach across his body. This time he had only to dive headlong with his glove outstretched and scoop the ball just before it hit the running track. Tommie Agee had done it again, had saved three runs, had taken the heart out of the Orioles' attack. ■

world series '69

Mets Drive Birds Cuckoo in 10, 2-1

by Phil Pepe

All the skeptics and cynics who wondered how a team like the Mets could win the National League pennant had only to show up at Shea Stadium yesterday to get their answer.

In winning a 2-1, 10-inning thriller from the Orioles in Game No. 4 of the World Series, the Mets shot the works and pulled out all of their particular talents—tough pitching and spectacular glove work on defense, a misjudged fly-ball double and a bad throw on offense.

The victory gives the Mets a 3-1 edge in games and leaves them one short of being crowned world champions in their eighth year of existence and with three chances to get it. Jerry Koosman, who beat the Birds in Game Two, gets a chance to wrap it up today against Dave McNally.

Unable to win in the regulation nine, the Mets used their best shots to win it in the frenetic 10th on a bunt by pinch-hitter J.C. Martin. When reliever Pete Richert fielded Martin's sac bunt and threw hurriedly to first, the ball struck Martin in the left wrist and bounded toward second as the winning run crossed the plate.

In answer to the question, "Who the hell is Rod Gaspar?" the Orioles will remember him as the Met who carried the winning run home.

Gaspar was on base as a runner for Jerry Grote, who led off the 10th

with a routine fly to short left. Don Buford, the Orioles' left fielder, misjudged the ball momentarily and started back to the fence.

When he realized the ball was not hit that far and changed direction, it was too late, and it plopped in short left out of reach of Buford, centerfielder, Paul Blair and shortstop Mark Belanger.

Gaspar's legs replaced Grote's legs at second and Oriole coach Billy Hunter ordered Al Weis intentionally walked to set up the force. Hunter was calling the shots because manager Earl Weaver was banished by plate ump Shag Crawford for protesting a called strike to Mark Belanger in the third.

Game 4 winner Tom Seaver gestures to the Orioles dugout.

Rod Gaspar jumps on home plate for the winning run as his teammates come out of the dugout to congratulate him.

Orioles were going to punch the clock for overtime.

When Boog Powell followed with a bouncing single through the right side, the Birds had runners on first and third with one out and Brooks Robinson batting.

Brooksie hit Seaver's first pitch hard to right, a sinking liner that looked like a double, good for one, maybe two runs. Charging hard, Ron Swoboda made a swan dive into the turf, his glove outstretched across his body, and the ball disappeared into the glove. It was a game-saver, if not a game-winner, as Frank Robby scored easily from third to tie it.

It was a daring try that would have cost the game if it had backfired, but Swoboda said he never thought about playing it safe in a situation like that.

"If I have one chance in 1,000 to catch the ball," Rocky said, "I'm going to try to catch it." ■

The way Seaver was pitching, it didn't look like there would be a 10th inning. This was the real Tom Seaver. This was the Tom Seaver who won 25 games during the regular season, not the Tom Seaver who was bombed by the Braves in the first playoff game and roughed up by the Orioles in the first game of this World Series.

Donn Clendenon had led off the second with a home run into the left field bullpen on Mike Cuellar's 3-2 pitch. It was Clendenon's second homer of the series and his fourth hit, three of them off Cuellar.

As Seaver nursed his 1-0 lead into the ninth, there was no indication that the

Ron Swoboda dives along the ground and grabs Brooks Robinson's line drive in the ninth inning at Shea Stadium.

world series '69

Sad Ending for Weaver

by Dana Mozley and Red Foley

*E*arl Weaver, like 60 million Americans, wound up watching the World Series on television yesterday. The spunky Orioles' manager had to resort to the boob tube after plate ump Shag Crawford thumbed him in the third inning following a prolonged beef over a called strike to Mark Belanger.*

Ejections are rare in a World Series game, the umpires being rather lenient in that respect. However, managers and players are usually warned about arguing and, in recent years, there have been very few beefs worth remembering.

When Weaver was thumbed, veteran newsmen were unable to recall the last time a manager got heaved in a series. Finally, someone came up with the fact that Cub manager Cholly Grimm got the gate in the 1935 series against Detroit. ∎

DAILY NEWS Dan Farrell

Umpire Shag Crawford points to the dugout after ejecting Orioles manager Earl Weaver in the third inning.

world series '69

Peace Leaflet Leaves Tom in Fighting Mood

by Dick Young

Tom Seaver threw hard and talked hard yesterday. He threw hard at the Orioles, and beat them. He talked hard against the presumptuous group of liberals, or radicals, or whatever they purport to be, for using his image on propaganda leaflets distributed outside Shea Stadium before the game. The leaflet bore his face in a Met cap, and the caption: Mets Fans for Peace.

"The people are being misled by that, and I resent it," said Tom Seaver. "I'm a ballplayer not a politician. I did not give them permission to use me.

"I have certain feelings on Vietnam, and I will express them as a U.S. citizen after this Series is all over."

That was after the game. Before the game, there were reactions to the pushiness of the moratorium leaders, including Mayor Lindsay.

The commissioner of baseball, too, had been used. He had been influenced by Mayor Lindsay at the ballgame the day before to proclaim baseball's support of the moratorium demonstrations. The U.S. flag in centerfield, Kuhn said, would be flown at half-staff during Game 4, at the request of the mayor. ∎

Commander James Fitzpatrick watches as his men thank Mr. Donald Grant, Mets board chairman, for giving World Series tickets to them and several hundred other Vietnam Vets.

world series '69

Hallelujah!
Mets Top the World

by Phil Pepe

o more worlds to conquer. No more miracles to perform. No more disbe-
lievers to convince. The Mets are world champions.

The eight-year-old, one-time ragamuffin, perennial doormat, not-to-be-believed Mets are the baseball champions of all the world and all the superlatives used when they won the National League Division title and the National League pennant can be trotted out again and they will still not be sufficient to describe the joy and the satisfaction of this world championship.

"What next?" said one sign the moment the Mets completed yesterday's 5-3 victory and became world champions and there was no answer, really, for the question.

"There are no words," said another sign and, indeed, it is difficult to put into words the extraordinary, incredible events of the last few hours, the last few days, the last few weeks, the last few months.

The Mets won it convincingly, four games to one over the American League Orioles, a so-called superteam which had won 109 of 162 games in its league, had won its division title by 19 games and had rolled through its playoff, as the Mets had, in a three-game sweep.

And the Mets won yesterday's clincher in typical Met fashion, refusing to quit when they fell behind, 3-0, and coming on to win with so many heroes that when it came time to name a series MVP there was support for five Mets.

When Cleon Jones gathered in Davey Johnson's drive at the warning track in left, it was the heart-pounding climax not of nine exciting innings, not of a remarkable year, it was the climax of eight frustration-filled years that began with Casey Stengel and ended with Gil Hodges. It was the fulfillment of a dream that began when the Dodgers and Giants moved out of New York in 1957 and now, a dozen years later, the Mets have won one more world championship than the San Francisco Giants.

And it was a victory that Ron Swoboda said as only Ron Swoboda can say, "will give heart to every loser in America."

In the end, they made Donn Clendenon the Most Valuable Player and it was a fitting choice because Donn Clendenon, like the Mets, represents a storybook rags-to-riches fable. When this season started, Donn Clendenon was working for an Atlanta pen company. Today, he is a World Series hero and there is no hero like a World Series hero.

They gave the MVP award to Donn Clendenon and it was fitting, but it would have been just as fitting—and just as deserved—if they had given it to Jerry Koosman, who was discovered pitching army ball and yesterday pitched the World Series clincher; or to Tommie Agee, who was a flop in 1968 and a team leader in 1969; or to Al Weis, who was cast off by the White Sox two years ago and hit the game-tying home run yesterday; or to Ron Swoboda, who lived through five years of frustration as a Met and yesterday knocked in the winning run with a double.

The Mets won it in the way they wanted to win it and they won it where they wanted to win it—in Shea Stadium. They did not want to return to Baltimore. They had seen Baltimore; there was no need to see it again.

But it seemed as if the return trip to Baltimore would be necessary when the Orioles' bats, silent throughout the last three games, finally exploded against Koosman in the third. The Orioles had abandoned their own style and did it the way the Mets do it, when Mark Belanger opened the third by popping a wrong-field single into right, so perfectly placed that Swoboda had no chance to make one of his flying trapeze catches.

Al Weis is welcomed to the dugout after his game-tying home run.

Pitcher Dave McNally followed by depositing Kooz' first pitch into the left field bullpen and was this the end of the age of miracles? Two outs later, Frank Robinson, who had been held to two singles and no ribbies in 16 at-bats, unloaded a tremendous home run over the left field bleachers.

McNally carried his 3-0 lead into the sixth and then the miracle worker awoke from his afternoon slumber. Cleon Jones was hit in the right foot by a pitch. That's what Cleon Jones said. That's what on-deck hitter Donn Clendenon said. And that's what Gil Hodges said. Plate ump Lou DiMuro said no, but Hodges produced the ball and showed DiMuro the mark of shoe polish right next to Warren Giles' signature and DiMuro was convinced. He waved Cleon to first.

The Orioles should have seen that as an omen. In the top half of the inning, Frank Robinson claimed he was hit in the side by a Koosman pitch. Earl Weaver thought so, too, but DiMuro said no and stayed with his decision. Robby struck out.

Clendenon followed Jones at bat. Naturally, he hit a 2-2 pitch into the second deck in left for his third series home run. The score was now 3-2. The miracle worker was doing his stuff. Al Weis led off the Mets' seventh. Al Weis, who had been cast aside by the White Sox in 1967. Al Weis, who has driven home only 23 runs all season. Al Weis, who had never hit a home run in Shea Stadium. Al Weis, who had hit two home runs all season, in successive games against the Cubs in Chicago back in July.

Al Weis came to bat and the sign man behind third base held up a sign that said: "Believe in miracles?" Then he held up another sign: "We

Donn Clendenon cut the Orioles' lead to 3-2 in the sixth inning of Game 5 with a two-run home run.

Game 5 winning pitcher Jerry Koosman jumps on his catcher Jerry Grote after Cleon Jones caught the fly out for the final out of the game.

believe." And Al Weis, who makes 165 on the scale when he has lead weights in each pocket, and who can't hit a ball that far, hit one into the leftfield bleachers, 375 feet away, to tie it, 3-3.

Jerry retired the Orioles in order in the eighth—he had allowed just one single since the third—and the Mets were coming to bat in the last of the eighth and throughout the stands there was that certain feeling.

Cleon Jones drove one off the centerfield fence for a double. Donn Clendenon couldn't bunt him over and rolled out to third, but Swoboda drove a hump-backed liner down the line in left.

Don Buford reached over and backhanded it . . . a trap, Jones scored the go-ahead run, Swoboda went to second and Shea Stadium was such bedlam you couldn't hear your watch ticking if you held it to your ear.

After Ed Charles flied to left, Jerry Grote rapped one down to first and the super defense of the super Orioles cracked again. Boog Powell bobbled it, then tossed too late to Watt covering and as Watt dropped the ball, Swoboda streaked around third and scored the insurance run. ■

World Series Game 5

	1	2	3	4	5	6	7	8	9	R	H	E
Orioles	0	0	3	0	0	0	0	0	0	3	5	2
Mets	0	0	0	0	0	2	1	2	x	5	7	0

Shoe-ing Birds, Mets Style

by Gene Ward

I t started out to be a day like all days. The dawn broke as dawns have been breaking for eons. The sun climbed into the sky and hid behind a full coverlet of clouds.

Three Oriole runs were in and Shea Stadium was so quiet you could hear the concession people chattering back in the areaways. Mrs. Payson carefully checked each item of her equipment to see what lucky charm she had forgotten.

Koosman picked McNally's first serve for a double in the bottom of the third, but Jerry died on second. The wind blew cold and Met fans who had come to Shea lightly clothed, with only their fervent faith to protect them, began to shiver.

The innings unraveled—the fourth, the fifth, then the bottom of the sixth, with little Cleon Jones leading off and getting hit on the shoe by a low McNally serve.

Plate ump Lou DiMuro said "no it didn't" and kept saying it until Gil Hodges came from the dugout, where the errant pitch had bounced, and showed him the shoe polish on the horsehide.

Little Cleon loped to first and Donn Clendenon sliced the Oriole bulge to 3-2 with his third homer of the Series into the leftfield bullpen.

A little bit of shoe polish had brought the Mets within a run of Baltimore.

You could almost sense the faith gushing back into the bodies of the Faithful.

Little Al Weis, leading off the bottom of the seventh, parked the first home run he ever hit in Shea on top of the wire screening which was stretched over the heads of the wounded Viet Nam vets seated behind the leftfield barricades.

The game was tied. Now the wind no longer was cold; Now the dark gray skies seemed laced with sunshine.

In the bottom of the eighth, it was Jones with a lead-off double . . . Swoboda with a double to left . . . Then the Birds became ruptured ducks as they committed a double error at first which permitted Swoboda to come barging all the way from second with the fifth run.

The greatest Mets' crowd in Shea history, 57,397 of them, held its collective breath on the very brink of its day-of-days. ∎

DAILY NEWS Ed Clarity

The championship banner flies over Shea.

Gil: Our Righty Platoon Did It; Casey: A Dynasty

October 17 , 1969
by Gil Hodges

You have to hand it to our righthanded platoon. They did it. The lefthanded team got us here, and now the righties have put the Mets on top of the baseball world. You can't be happier for a Clendenon, a Weis, a Swoboda.

You have to remember Swoboda did it with a righthander pitching at the end. That's supposed to be pitching to our weakness, and he just pops a double down the line.

Some of the writers asked if in a spot like that, and sending up Shamsky, I thought about taking Swoboda out for another lefhanded hitter. I'll tell you the things that go through a manager's mind at the time:

Cleon gets a double to lead off the inning. You want Clendenon to bunt, but he fouled it off and you don't get the man over. Even if he did, Swoboda still hits for us, because if I send up a lefthander they probably put him on, and that brings up Ed Charles, another member of our righty platoon.

If we put in another lefty for Charles, they bring in a lefthanded pitcher. So, you add all these things up and you decide to stick with Swoboda, because you know what he can do. You know how he has come through before against a righthander.

October 17, 1969
by Casey Stengel

The night they clinched I said they's a Mets dynasty that will last 10 years this century. They come from behind by runnin' out the ball and hittin' it over the fences which the manager platoons them amazin'ly that he has one old team on the bench and a young team on the bench and they all come through for him.

This wasn't a two-man pitchin' staff it's a six-man staff which has three good relief pitchers that you get out when you need the groundball. I said they'd win which I know Baltimore's a good team they hadn't played in three weeks.

DAILY NEWS John Duprey

Gentry, Gaspar and Garrett

Garrett is Mets' Bargain of the Year

by Dick Young

> "I wanted it for myself, but now I know I can't. I think my roomie has a good shot at it. So does Red."

Rod Gaspar was talking about Rookie of the Year. His roomie is Gary Gentry. Red is Wayne Garrett and if he doesn't win Rookie of the Year, he's a cinch for Bargain of the Season. The Mets picked him out of the regular draft last December for $25,000 and you don't hardly get those kind anymore.

Gary Gentry is the Mets' pitcher of this year. Each year, they've come up with a dandy. In 1967, it was Tom Seaver. In '68, Jerry Koosman. In 1969, Gary Gentry.

"Two more," says Gil Hodges, "and some of the hitters in the league might worry about coming into Shea."

"It's considered a good year," says Tom Seaver, the precocious philosopher, "when a club comes up with one or two outstanding rookies. We've come up with three."

There is a contributing circumstance, sometimes overlooked. An expansion draft was held. Holes opened on all rosters. Replacements were needed. It is a bullish market for a rookie.

"Gentry would have made the club anyway, I think," says Gil Hodges.

It happens occasionally. A kid comes to camp with the credentials. He's a cinch, unless he drowns in the Gulf of Mexico. He has the minor league record, and the can't-miss scouting reports. His reputation has preceded him. "He had to pitch himself off the club, not onto it," says Rube Walker, who regulates the Mets' pitchers.

Gary Gentry had only a year and a half in the minors when they decided he was ready to start in the bigs, but he also had pitched at Arizona State, where they develop more good ballplayers than most farm systems. Gentry pitched State to the collegiate title in '67 with a 17-and-1 record.

Rod Gaspar was the surprise Met. Few people expected him to make the club. He hustled himself onto the team. He was a switch hitter, a good bunter, an exciting baserunner, and he covered acres of ground in the outfield.

Wayne Garrett is a Met because of two people, Bob Scheffing and Charley Lau. Make that three. The guy around the block who knocked Garrett down during a touch-tackle game counts, too.

It was after the 1966 season in the Florida State League. Red Garrett had taken his Army physical, got a bristling 1A and was waiting around to be called. They chose up a game of touch football, and it got a little rough as usual. Garrett went up for a pass. The guy went up with him. There was a mid-air tangle and Garrett landed flat on his back, his left leg pinned grotesquely under him.

At the hospital, they said he had torn some back muscles and cracked a couple of vertebrae, and the Army changed the 1A to 1Y. They call him back occasionally for a recheck.

The Braves, who owned him, sent Red Garrett to the Arizona Instructional League last winter, and that's where Bob Scheffing came in. Scheffing is the Mets' man in Arizona.

"This kid came fast in the last month down there," recalled Scheffing. "The thing that impressed me was he was hitting the better pitchers. He was going to all fields. We needed infielders and I thought he'd be worth a draft."

Red Garrett, Rod Gaspar, Gary Gentry—all have helped the Mets climb. "We need a few more," says Gil Hodges. "Then we'll be a solid club."

The Mets have had an exciting glimpse at winning, just a taste. As Ed Kranepool said it:

"Something is happening. Any young fellow who gets with the Mets right now is in on the verge of something about to explode."

Tips for a Rookie

Keep your cool. No matter what happens to shake you up, try to forget it and look ahead. That's the toughest thing for a young fellow to do. Be patient. I've had trouble with that. I'd get mad at myself, disgusted with myself. Everybody does. But when you're out there and things are going against you, what you should do is think about what's next, not what you did last.

—Gary Gentry

Winning pitcher Jerry Koosman (36) and catcher Jerry Grote kick off New York's celebration of the Mets' World Championship.

Celebration
'69

After all the baseball titles racked up by the Dodgers and Yankees, it would be understandable if New York City was blasé about a World Championship.

But the city went wild with spontaneous celebration after the New York Mets won the World Series in five games, winning four straight. The Mets were at the pinnacle of baseball after years of humiliation. They made the most of it. The celebration brought Times Square to a halt and the East Side, too.

And this was all before the city turned out to officially celebrate the Mets' championship with a proper ticker-tape parade.

World Champion City Is Wild!

by Arthur Mulligan

ever before—not for the onetime perennial world champion Yankees, not for the moon men, not for Charles A. Lindbergh, not for anyone. Never before had New Yorkers exploded in quite the way they did yesterday in a spontaneous, unrestrained outpouring of sheer joy when the Mets, their Mets, copped the World Series.

From Montauk to Morrisania and points beyond, a collective shout of exultant ecstasy went up. People screamed wildly from windows, strangers embraced on the streets, ticker tape and confetti the like of which has never been seen before showered into the streets from downtown to midtown.

A *News* reporter at 40th St. and Madison Ave. said that Fifth Ave. was blanketed with the stuff "both north and south, as far as the eye could see."

This was utter Metsomania, that happy malaise which gripped New Yorkers eight years ago when the fumbling, befuddled infant Mets were born, the Mets that Casey Stengel so aptly asked of once: "Can't anybody here play this game?"

DAILY NEWS Dennis Caruso

Mets manager Gil Hodges takes a congratulatory call from President Richard M. Nixon after winning the World Series.

This was the fruition, the culmination, the climax, the unbelievable triumph of the once hapless Mets after all these years of frustration. This was heaven and New Yorkers made the most of it.

They left their offices and homes to dance in the streets and atop parked vehicles. Elderly ladies, who might be considered unlikely to have ever heard of the Mets, clutched their pocketbooks above their heads with both hands and shouted their praise.

Pretty girls in miniskirts kissed everyone in sight. The excitement grew as the first shock of unbelievable fulfillment gave way to ever increasing frenzy. It was a town—the Big Town—gone mad.

As the celebration grew in intensity, traffic in Times Square and on the East Side came almost to a halt. People snake-danced in the gutters and reduced vehicle traffic in some places to one moving lane in each direction. Extra police were sent to the Wall Street area to try to keep a semblance of sanity and order there. ■

OPPOSITE: Met fans dance in the street on 44th St. between Third and Lexington. The spontaneous celebration brought traffic to a standstill all over New York City.

Celebration '69

5 Shea Fans Hospitalized

Victory Hysteria Nearly Turns to Bedlam

by Wes Gaffer and Tom Pugh

Drs. Jon Wang and Michael Kohen of Roosevelt Hospital, on special duty at the ballpark, treated 31 victims of the fan hysteria that erupted yesterday at Shea Stadium before the last putout was made. Five of the victims were sent to Booth Memorial Hospital, two with possible fractures of the heel and one with a broken jaw.

One of the hospitalized wounded was usher Bob Mathews, who was thrown from the roof of the dugout. Another unidentified man also was thrown off the roof. The man with the fractured jaw had tried to steal home plate during a melee that saw *News* photographer Frank Giorandino have his camera taken away from him and *News* cameraman John Duprey knocked to the ground by stadium specials.

The specials tried to drag Duprey into a small room under the stands where they reportedly threatened to beat him. Only the intervention of a police captain saved the photographer. Said Dr. Wang to an inquiring reporter, "If you really want to see a kid with a broken heart, go next door." Next door was a large, temporary headquarters for the tactical and special events police.

There, 16-year-old John Mucia, a student at Fort Hamilton HS, was sobbing.

Mets fans wear their hunks of Shea Stadium's turf as they head home.

celebration '69

"They took it from me. They wouldn't let me have it," he sobbed over and over again.

Before the last out was made, the horde flushed down the aisles and swamped the field, storming the dugout and the playing area. The press of human bodies was so great that the aisles could no longer accommodate them and they climbed over the top of the boxes.

The specials were able to ease the enormous pressure by resorting somewhat crazily but effectively to an incredibly normal practice. They would open the gates and say "four at a time" and let them pass.

Surprisingly it worked. It also bought time for the Mets' official party to scurry under official guard to the safety of the clubhouse. ■

DAILY NEWS

RIGHT: Ron Swoboda and Tommie Agee, who made three crucial catches between them, celebrate their World Series championship.
BELOW: World Series heroes (l to r) Ed Kranepool, Gary Gentry, Tommie Agee and Nolan Ryan celebrate a World Series victory.

DAILY NEWS John Duprey

celebration '69

From a Grateful City. . . Thanks, Mets

by Phil Pepe

*I*t was a championship for a city in turmoil, a city starving for a winner. It was a championship that brought special people together again, made them forget their personal differences and unified them in a spirit of camaraderie to pull for the Mets and to exult in their triumph that belonged to each one of us.

It was a championship that united New Yorkers against Baltimoreans and the big, cold city dropped its facade of sophistication to gloat in victory. First the Jets, then the Knicks, now the Mets. Who owns New York? The Mets own New York. Who owns Baltimore? The Mets own Baltimore.

"New York is a sports town once again," a man said and that told it all.

As the big town awoke yesterday, pinched itself and began to dig its way out of an avalanche of ticker tape, confetti and mounds of paper that resembled the aftermath of the big snow of 1947, plans were under way to honor its latest heroes. ∎

Mets owner Mrs. Joan Payson shows off her copy of the Daily News from the day of her team's World Championship.

New York City mayor John Lindsay holds up a street sign designating a block at Bedford Ave., where Hodges lives, "Gil Hodges Place" for a day.

Yes, Mets, It Was for Real

October 21, 1969

"There are more people here on one street corner than in my whole home town. This is just incredible."

That is the way Jim McAndrew, a 25-year-old Met pitcher from Lost Nation, Iowa (pop. 537), described "the biggest day in my life."

"I've seen things like this on TV but never realized how it would be until now," he said while he was patted, pawed and greeted by thousands of fans as he rode up Broadway. "But the full impact hasn't sunk in yet. I don't think I'll ever get over it."

Wayne Garrett, the youngest of the Mets at 21, was equally moved. "I've never seen anything like this, nor could I ever have imaged anything like this could happen," he remarked as he combed the confetti out of his red hair.

Ed Kranepool, the only home-bred Met, from the Bronx, said: "I have never seen such a large and enthusiastic crowd. But the fans deserve this day. They are the No. 1 fans in the No. 1 town in the world."

Those Hail-Fellows Very Well Met!

City Gives Its Heart to the Lovables

by William Travers and Arthur Mulligan

They said it couldn't be done. That a city drained of every happy emotion following the Mets' amazing World Series victory Thursday could rise again to the occasion with the same lusty outpouring of admiration and joy. But they underestimated New Yorkers—just as they had underestimated the Mets.

The Amazin' Ones took New York by storm yesterday just as they had taken Chicago, Atlanta and Baltimore, but in this case it was a pleasure for those who were taken, the Mets' own fans. It was the day of the city's official tribute to the newest New York world champs—and the populace roared its acclaim once again as if the Mets' miraculous victory were only minutes old.

From the moment the motorcade started, crowds surged from behind police barricades and pressed forward through ankle-deep ticker tape and confetti to greet their warriors. They tried to shake their hands and touch their sleeves. Many young girls bestowed kisses on their heroes.

Ecstatic youngsters, and older persons too, tried to climb onto and into the convertibles as they moved slowly up Broadway.

It was a wild crowd, but a happy one, and police assigned along the route let it have its head. There were no attempts to interfere with the fun.

Some 5,000 persons thronged City Hall Plaza as the entourage arrived there shortly before noon.

The Mayor presented the keys of the city to Mrs. Joan Payson, owner of the Mets, and Don Grant, board chairman of the champs. Lindsay gave manager Gil Hodges the city's bronze medallion and a replica of a street sign designating the block on Bedford Ave., Brooklyn, where Hodges lives, 'Gil Hodges Place' for the day. ■

OPPOSITE:
Top: World Champion N.Y. Mets' Tom Seaver and Jerry Koosman greet Met fans during the ticker-tape parade on the way to City Hall.

Bottom: Ralph Andretta, 8, of Brooklyn toots his horn for the World Champion Mets at City Hall.

celebration '69

Epilogue

The 1969 season changed all of our lives. Make no mistake about that. Those of us from that team who still live in the New York Metropolitan area are reminded every day in some manner about that year by people young and old. Countless fans have vivid memories of the events of that year, but what I find really interesting is that children and grandchildren who weren't even born in 1969 know about that team from their parents and their grandparents. This is what legacies are made of. Perhaps the stories are embellished a little, but no one cares. It doesn't even matter if all the facts are correct. The only thing that matters is that a group of guys went from "lovable losers" to "World Champions" and gave our city, the country, and many around the world reason to rejoice.

Over the years, all of the players and coaches have remained very close. Of course, it helped to be a part of that wonderful experience. But, it truly was a team made up of unselfish people who respected each other on and off the field. To list all of the things that have happened to us as a team since 1969 would take pages and pages. We've been celebrating for 30 years. Other books have been written about the '69 Mets and countless tributes have taken place over the years. In fact, in 1994 for the 25th Anniversary, the players and coaches decided to form a corporation together to market ourselves and raise money for charities. It also gave us an opportunity to interact with our fans in a series of events. Over 30 products were produced for the retail market such as T-shirts, caps, pins, limited edition postcards, trading card sets and telephone calling cards, to name a few.

In the strike-shortened season of 1994, the 1969 Mets were still able to raise over one million dollars for charities such as The Muscular Dystrophy Association, The Leukemia Society, and The Make a Wish Foundation. Think for a moment. What team could market itself 30 years after a World Championship? The fact of the matter is that we did it, and today, the team has as much popularity now as it did in 1969. In fact, maybe more.

With the 30th Anniversary upon us, we remain as strong and as united as ever. Most of the players continue to make personal appearances, and collectively as a team, we are available for corporate functions and special events.

Make no mistake about it, I believe that the 1969 Miracle Mets will live forever and the legacy will live on and on.

Other championship teams will come and go, but none will remain immortalized in so many people's hearts. The cast of characters that made up the team, against the backdrop of the events of that year that are indelibly etched in our nation's collective conscience, has long since made this team special in so many ways. History will show that while the 1969 Mets might not have been the greatest team to win a World Championship, we certainly and unmistakably are one of the most memorable.

Art Shamsky

If you would like to contact the 1969 Mets for corporate functions and special events, call (718) 460-4921.

1969 Mets (l to r) Ed Kranepool, Tommie Agee, Bud Harrelson, Ed Charles, Tom Seaver and Art Shamsky.

The 1969 New York Mets

Player	AB	H	2B	3B	BA	SA	HR	RBI	SB
Tommie Agee	565	153	23	4	.271	.464	26	76	12
Ken Boswell	362	101	14	7	.279	.381	3	32	7
Ed Charles	169	35	8	1	.207	.320	3	18	4
Donn Clendenon	202	51	11	1	.252	.432	12	37	3
Duffy Dyer	74	19	3	1	.257	.446	3	12	0
Wayne Garrett	400	87	11	3	.218	.268	1	39	4
Rod Gaspar	215	49	6	1	.228	.279	1	14	7
Jerry Grote	365	92	12	3	.252	.351	6	40	2
Bud Harrelson	395	98	11	6	.248	.306	0	24	1
Cleon Jones	483	164	25	4	.340	.482	12	75	16
Ed Kranepool	353	84	9	2	.238	.368	11	49	3
J.C. Martin	177	37	5	1	.209	.316	4	21	0
Bobby Pfeil	211	49	9	0	.232	.275	0	10	0
Art Shamsky	303	91	9	3	.300	.488	14	47	1
Ron Swoboda	327	77	10	2	.235	.361	9	52	1
Al Weis	247	53	9	2	.215	.291	2	23	3

Pitcher	Games	Innings	Won	Lost	Saved	ERA
Tom Seaver	36	273	25	7	0	2.21
Jerry Koosman	32	241	17	9	0	2.28
Gary Gentry	35	234	13	12	0	3.43
Don Cardwell	30	152	8	10	0	3.01
Jim McAndrew	27	135	6	7	0	3.47
Tug McGraw	42	100	9	3	12	2.24
Nolan Ryan	25	89	6	3	1	3.53
Cal Koonce	40	83	6	3	7	4.99
Ron Taylor	59	76	9	4	13	2.72
Jack DiLauro	23	63	1	4	1	2.39

Other DAILY NEWS Titles

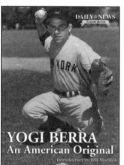

Yogi Berra: An American Original

This book represents the most complete collection of Yogi Berra materials ever published, including rarely seen pictures from his early years in Yankee pinstripes, to his World Series heroics on the great Yankee teams of the 1950s and early 1960s, through his ups and downs as manager and coach of the tradition-rich Yankees and the upstart Mets, and concluding with his life after baseball.
218 pp • 8 1/2 x 11 hardcover • $29.95

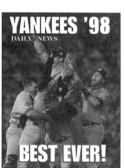

Yankees '98: Best Ever

This full-color retrospective commemorates the entire 1998 Yankees season from the pre-season arrival of El Duque, to David Wells' perfect game, to the Yankees' unprecedented achievements throughout the post season. This book includes week-by-week review of the season, complete post season box scores, player profiles and much more.
156 pp • 8 1/2 x 11 paperback • $19.95

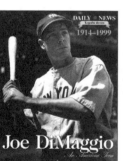

Joe DiMaggio: An American Icon

This Legend Series title covers Joe's entire baseball career plus the public aspects of his relationships with Marilyn Monroe, his family and his life after baseball. **192 pp • 8 1/2 x 11 hardcover • $29.95**

Jets: Broadway's 30-Year Guarantee

This publication takes fans back to relive the Jets' 1968 season and their astonishing Namath-guaranteed 16-7 triumph in the 1969 Super Bowl. Each game of that season of destiny is recounted including in-depth coverage of Super Bowl III retelling of New York's most memorable day in sports. Foreword by Hall of Famer Don Maynard.
192 pp • 8 1/2 x 11 hardcover • $29.95

Jets: Broadway's 30-Year Guarantee leatherbound $99.95

Limited edition of 500
Signed by: **Don Maynard**
          Larry Grantham
          Matt Snell
          Gerry Philbin
          George Sauer

Big Town Big Time

From Typhoid Mary to the opening of Yankee Stadium to the unforgettable blackout, it's a time to remember. Including *The Luckiest Man on the Face of the Earth-Lou Gehrig Day 1939*, and *And Sometimes Connect-The Babe Comes Back, 1923*. *Big Town Big Time* is the colorful panoply of politics, culture, crime, sports, etc....The personalities, the events, the flow of time.
198 pp • 9 1/2 x 13 hardcover • $39.95

Available at your local bookstore or by calling toll free 877-424-2665

Timeless Classics...

The Amazin' Mets
and the United States
Postal Service

**UNITED STATES
POSTAL SERVICE.**